Collins

Geography

KS3

KS3

Geography

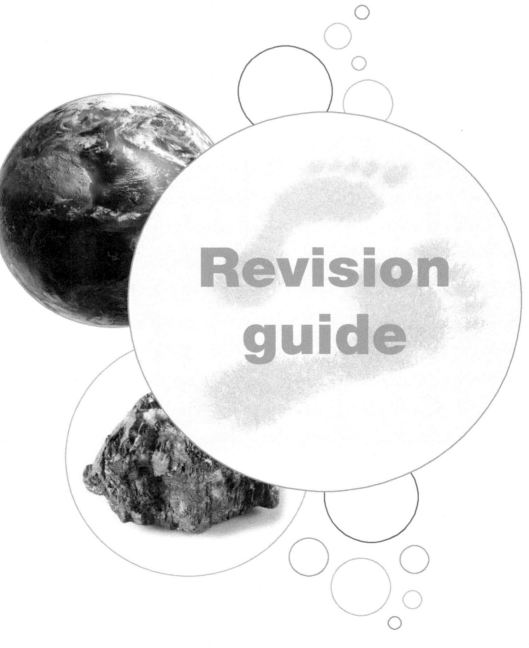

Revision guide

David Rayner, Andrew Browne & Victoria Turner

Contents

Contents

Location Knowledge – Russia

You must be able to:

- Describe the environmental regions of Russia
- Understand the key physical and human characteristics of Russia
- Name the major cities of Russia.

Environmental Regions

- **Tundra** is found in the far north of Russia. Temperatures can fall to as low as –50°C in the winter. Trees cannot grow because it is too cold and the ground is frozen all year round (**permafrost**).
- **Taiga** is a region of coniferous trees such as pine, spruce and fir that covers approximately 60% of Russia.
- **Steppe** is a region of grassland plains south of the taiga. The climate is too dry for forests to grow but the soil, known as **chernozem**, is very fertile and good for agriculture.
- **Semi-arid** deserts are located in the far south of Russia where summer temperatures can reach over 38°C and total annual rainfall is less than 250 mm.
- **Deciduous** forests containing oak, ash, birch and beech trees are found in the west of Russia.

Key Point

All of the major climate zones can be found in Russia, apart from tropical.

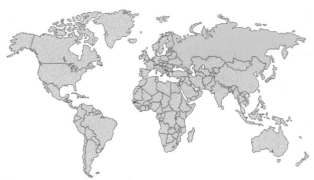

Physical and Human Characteristics

- Russia is the largest country in the world. It is 1.8 times larger than the USA and covers over 17 million km².
- Russia's main river is the Volga which is 3692 km long (making it Europe's longest river).
- The Urals mountain range runs north to south across Western Russia. It creates a boundary between European Russia and Siberia, a region consisting mainly of cold steppe and tundra covering 77% of Russia.
- Russia's highest mountain is Mt Elbrus (5642 m) in the Caucasus Mountains, which mark the border between Southern Russia and Georgia.
- Russia has many **natural resources** including natural gas, oil, coal, iron ore, timber and gold. The total potential value of Russia's resources is estimated to be $30 trillion.
- There are 15 cities in Russia with a population of 1 million or more. The capital of Russia is Moscow which has a population of over 11 million. Russia's second city is St Petersburg with a population of nearly 5 million.

Tundra

Taiga

- The population of Russia has declined from 149 million in 1991 to 143 million in 2013. Following the collapse of the Soviet Union in 1991 the uncertain future of their country made Russians reluctant to have large families. *[handwritten: ? reinstate]*
- Russia has the eighth largest economy in the world. Russia's main industries are in manufacturing such as defence and motor vehicles. High-tech industries, including information technology, nanotechnology and the space industry, are growing rapidly.
- Vladimir Putin has been the president of Russia since 2000. In that time the economy has grown on average by 7% a year, people's incomes have doubled and the percentage of people living in poverty has fallen from 30% to 14% of the population.
- In 2014 Russia hosted the Winter Olympics in Sochi, on the north east coast of the Black Sea. It cost Russia $51 billion to stage making it the most expensive Olympic Games in history.

Development Indicators for Russia	
Gross Domestic Product (GDP) (per capita)	$17 500
Employment Structure: Primary Secondary Tertiary	8% 27% 65%
Life Expectancy	70 years
Adult Literacy	99.7%
Human Development Index (HDI)	0.788 (55th out of 187 countries)

Moscow

> ### Key Point
>
> Today, even though the economy is growing, rising childcare costs and a desire to concentrate on their careers mean people are still choosing to have fewer children.

Steppe

Quick Test

1. Which type of environmental region covers the majority of Russia?
2. What is the frozen ground found in tundra regions known as?
3. Name Russia's longest river.
4. What is the population of Russia's second largest city?

Key Words

tundra
permafrost
taiga
steppe
chernozem
semi-arid
deciduous
natural resources

Location Knowledge – China

You must be able to:

- Describe the environmental regions of China
- Understand the key physical and human characteristics of China
- Name the major cities of China.

Environmental Regions

- Taiga (coniferous forests) and steppe (grasslands) are found in north-east China including the Manchurian Plain, which covers an area of 350 000 km².
- The North China Plain is a lowland area in eastern China that covers an area of 409 500 km². Here there is a sub-tropical monsoon climate with cold, dry winters and hot, wet summers. This is a major agricultural region where wheat, cotton, peanuts, tea, rice and tobacco are grown.
- Tropical rainforest is found in south-east China. On Hainan island, China's southern-most point, over 3000 species of plants and more than 4700 species of animal have been recorded.
- North-west China contains two major cold deserts, the Gobi desert and the Taklamakan desert. The Gobi desert is 1.3 million km², temperatures can vary from as low as –40°C to as high as 40°C and it receives an average of 194 mm of precipitation a year (some of it falling as snow).
- The Tibetan Plateau is in south-west China. It is over 4500 m above sea level and covers 2.5 million km² (four times the area of France). It is an area of alpine tundra characterised by grasses and low shrubs, with wildlife such as bears, marmots and yak.

Physical and Human Characteristics

- China is the third largest country in the world covering an area of 9.6 million km².
- The longest river in China is the Yangtze. It is 6300 km long, making it the third longest river in the world after the Nile and the Amazon.
- China has 1500 rivers that drain catchment areas of over 1000 km².
- North and north-west China is in a major earthquake zone; on 12 May 2008 the Sichuan Earthquake struck. At 8 on the Richter scale, it was the 21st deadliest earthquake ever recorded; 87 000 were killed and 374 000 injured.
- China has the largest population in the world, with approximately 1.3 billion people in 2013.

Key Point

Mt Everest, the tallest mountain in the world at 8848 m, is located on the border of Nepal and China.

Rice Farming

Key Point

The **One Child Policy** was introduced in 1979 to control the rapid growth of China's population; the policy was successful in reducing the number of births by approximately 400 million between 1979 and 2009.

- There are over 600 cities in China and more than 150 of these have a population of at least a million:
  - The largest city in China is Chongqing (28.84 million)
  - Shanghai has 23.01 million
  - The capital, Beijing, has 19.61 million
  - Tianjin has 12.93 million.
- China is the world's second largest economy, after the USA. China's economy has been growing rapidly at an average rate of 10% a year since the 1980s. Manufacturing and construction dominate the Chinese economy.
- China is a Communist country with only one political party, the Communist Party. The government used to own and control all the agriculture and industry, but since 1978 the government has allowed people to own and run their own businesses.

Development Indicators for China	
Gross Domestic Product (GDP) (per capita)	$9100
Employment Structure: Primary Secondary Tertiary	 35% 29% 36%
Life Expectancy	75 years
Adult Literacy	95.1%
Human Development Index (HDI)	0.699 (101st out of 187 countries)

Shanghai

> **Key Point**
>
> China is the world's largest importer and exporter of goods.

Gobi Desert

Alpine tundra

> **Key Words**
>
> sub-tropical
> tropical rainforest
> cold desert
> alpine tundra
> catchment area
> One Child Policy
> earthquake
> Richter scale
> manufacturing
> Communist

Quick Test

1. Name three crops grown in China.
2. How many births did the One Child Policy prevent between 1979 and 2009?
3. Name the longest river in China and give its length.
4. Which political party is in power in China?

Location Knowledge – India

You must be able to:

- Describe the environmental regions of India
- Understand the key physical and human characteristics of India
- Name the major cities of India.

Environmental Regions

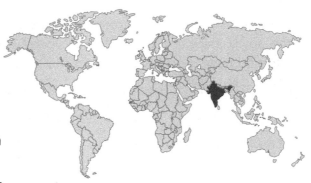

- The Himalayas have an alpine tundra climate where snow lies on the ground all year round.
- The Indo-Gangetic Plain in the north of India has a humid sub-tropical climate with hot, wet summers and cold, dry winters. It is 700 000 km² and was formed from the sediments of the rivers that flow from the Himalayas. Thick forests grow here and the region is farmed for rice, wheat, maize, sugar cane and cotton.
- The Thar Desert is a hot desert found in north-west India. It is over 200 000 km² and temperatures range from 5°C in the winter to 50°C in the summer.
- The Deccan Plateau rises approximately 600 m above sea level and covers 1.3 million km² of central and southern India. It is a semi-arid region with vegetation that varies from thorn bushes to forests and wildlife including tigers and Indian elephants. Tea and coffee plantations are found on the Deccan Plateau.
- The Western Ghats, on the west coast of southern India, have a tropical wet climate where temperatures do not fall below 18°C and tropical forests grow.

The Himalayas

Physical and Human Characteristics

- India is the seventh largest country in the world covering 3 287 263 km².
- India has a monsoon climate with four seasons:
   Winter: December to March.
  2 Summer (dry season): April to June.
  3 Monsoon (rainy season): July to September.
  4 Autumn: October to November.
- India has three major rivers: the Indus (3180 km), which flows through Pakistan, Tibet and India; the Ganges (2525 km), which flows through India and Bangladesh; and the Brahmaputra (2900 km), which flows through Tibet, India and Bangladesh.
- By 2025 India will have the world's third largest economy after the USA and China. Major Indian industries include motor vehicles, shipbuilding, chemicals, telecommunications, computers and software development.

Key Point

Over 80% of people in India are Hindus, 13% are Muslim, 2% are Christian and the remaining 5% are mainly Sikh or Buddhist.

Key Point

Despite wages doubling between 2000 and 2010, 25% of India's population still live on less than $1.25 a day.

- The population of India in 2013 was 1.27 billion people, making India the second most populous country in the world after China.
- There are nearly 50 cities in India with a population of 1 million or more. According to India's last census in 2011 the largest city in India is Mumbai (12 478 447) followed by the capital Delhi (11 007 835) and Bangalore (8 425 970).
- India used to be part of the British Empire but gained its independence from Britain in 1947 under the leadership of Jawaharlal Nehru. India is now the world's largest democracy with six main political parties and general elections held every five years.

Development Indicators for India	
Gross Domestic Product (GDP) (per capita)	$4000
Employment Structure: Primary Secondary Tertiary	53% 19% 28%
Birth Rate (per 1000) Death Rate (per 1000) Natural Increase (per 1000)	20.9 7.5 12.8
Life Expectancy	67.5 years
Adult Literacy	62.8%
Human Development Index (HDI)	0.554 (136th out of 187 countries)

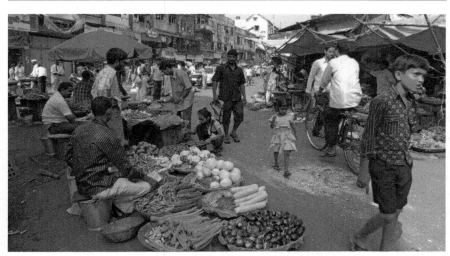
Mumbai

Key Point

India's population is expected to overtake China's by 2030 when it will reach an estimated 1.53 billion people.

Western Ghat

Thar Desert

Key Words

alpine tundra
humid sub-tropical
hot desert
semi-arid
tropical wet
monsoon
British Empire
independence
democracy

Quick Test

1. Name the type of environment found in the Himalayas.
2. When does India's rainy season (monsoon) take place?
3. Which is the longest river that flows through India?
4. When did India gain its independence from the British Empire?

Location Knowledge – The Middle East

You must be able to:

- Describe the environmental regions of the Middle East
- Understand the key physical and human characteristics of the Middle East
- Name the major cities of the Middle East.

Environmental Regions

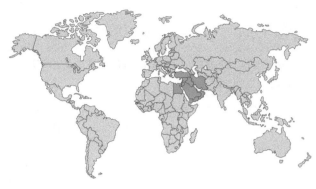

- Most of the Middle East is hot desert. This includes the Egyptian section of the Sahara Desert and the Arabian Desert, which covers 2.3 million km^2 of the Arabian Peninsula.
- The Arabian Desert includes the Rub' al Khali or 'Empty Quarter' which, at 650 000 km^2, is the largest sand desert in the world, with 250 m high sand dunes. Rainfall here is less than 30 mm a year.
- Western Turkey has a Mediterranean climate characterised by warm wet winters and hot dry summers. Typical Mediterranean vegetation includes pine, cedar, olive and citrus trees, and shrubs and bushes such as lavender and rosemary.

Physical and Human Characteristics

- The Middle East is an area of mainly West Asian countries located between Africa, Europe and Central Asia.
- The Middle East covers an area of 13 million km^2 and has a population of approximately 350 million. High population densities are found near sources of water (rivers and lakes).
- A number of narrow waterways carry trade into and out of the Middle East, including the Suez Canal linking the Mediterranean Sea to the Red Sea; Bab el Mandeb, a strait that separates the Red Sea from the Indian Ocean; and the Strait of Hormuz, linking the Persian Gulf and the Indian Ocean.
- The three largest rivers in the Middle East are the Nile in Egypt (6650 km), the Euphrates that flows through Turkey, Syria and Iraq (2800 km) and the Tigris, which flows through Turkey and joins the Euphrates in Iraq (1850 km).
- 60% of the population are Arabs, an ethnic group from the Arabian Peninsula, who speak Arabic. Other important ethnic groups in the Middle East are Persians, Turks, Kurds and Jews (the latter make up 85% of the population of Israel).

(handwritten: ? West Bank and Gaza)

Key Point

The countries of the Middle East are: Bahrain, Cyprus, Egypt, Iran, Iraq, Israel, Jordan, Kuwait, Lebanon, Oman, Palestine, Qatar, Saudi Arabia, Syria, Turkey, United Arab Emirates and Yemen.

(handwritten: 17)

Arabian Desert, UAE

- Islam is the main religion in the majority of Middle Eastern countries and most Muslims follow the Sunni sect of Islam. There are significant numbers of Christians in Lebanon, Egypt and Israel.
- The total annual **Gross Domestic Product (GDP)** in the Middle East was $4.3 trillion in 2012. But the GDP of individual countries ranged from $2000 per capita in Iraq to $68 000 per capita in Qatar.
- The largest cities in the Middle East are:
  - Istanbul in Turkey (14 million)
  - Cairo in Egypt (9 million)
  - Tehran in Iran (8 million)
  - Baghdad in Iraq (6 million)
  - Riyadh and Jeddah in Saudi Arabia both have populations of 5 million.

Iraq
Iran

Key Point

The richest countries of the Middle East gain their wealth from exporting oil. These countries include Qatar, Bahrain, the United Arab Emirates, Kuwait, Saudi Arabia, and Oman.

Development Indicators for the Middle East	
Gross Domestic Product (GDP) (per capita)	$7.112
Birth Rate (per 1000)	23.3
Death Rate (per 1000)	5.4
Natural Increase (per 1000)	17.9
Life Expectancy	70.1 years
Adult Literacy	83.8%
Human Development Index (HDI)	Israel 0.900–Yemen 0.458

Cairo

Suez Canal

Dubai

Quick Test

1. How large is the Arabian Desert?
2. What is special about the Rub' al Khali?
3. Which is the largest ethnic group in the Middle East?
4. Name two religions practised in the Middle East.

Key Words

Mediterranean climate
Arab
ethnic group
Gross Domestic Product (GDP)

Africa and Asia Compared – Kenya

You must be able to:

- Describe and explain the physical and human geography of Kenya
- Understand the similarities and differences between Kenya and other places
- Understand the links between Kenya and other places.

Physical Characteristics

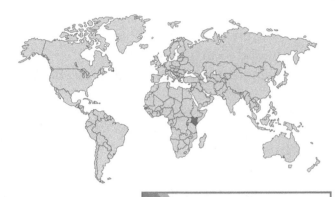

- Kenya covers an area of 582 650 km^2, more than twice the area of the UK.
- Kenya is on the equator giving it a tropical climate where the sun stays overhead all year.
- Kenya has two rainy seasons: the 'long rains' from April to June and the 'short rains' from October to December. Total annual rainfall for Kenya is 1390 mm (similar to the UK's).
- The hot dry season is from January to March (average temperature 29°C) and the cool dry season is from July to September (average temperature 26°C).
- Being on the equator also means that the times of sunrise and sunset stay the same all year (6:00–6:30am and 6:30–7:00pm).
- Kenya has five main environmental zones:
  1. Steppe, consisting of desert-like scrub and grassland, covering most of the north and east.
  2. Hot desert in the far north.
  3. Tropical equatorial forest on the east coast.
  4. Savannah grasslands covering the south.
  5. Montane forest in the Kenyan Highlands of Western Kenya (tropical evergreen forests with high temperatures and humidity, and high densities of orchids, ferns, mosses and lichen).
- Kenya's highest mountain is Mt Kenya at 5119 m. It is a stratovolcano, formed over three million years ago.
- The Great Rift Valley runs through the west of Kenya. It is being formed as the African tectonic plate splits in two and has been partially filled by lakes such as Lake Turkana.

Human Characteristics

- The population of Kenya was 44 million in 2013.
- Kenya has a very young population, with over 60% of the population under the age of 25 and only 6% over the age of 55. In the UK, 29% are over 55.
- Annual population growth in Kenya is 2.27%, which means an extra million people in Kenya each year.

Key Point

The savannah is the most well-known environmental region in Kenya. It consists of vast plains of grass with scattered trees such as the baobab and acacia. The savannah is where the majority of Kenya's wildlife is to be found, such as giraffe, lion, elephant, leopard, cheetah, hippo and rhinoceros.

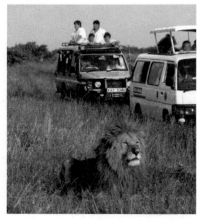

On safari

- Kenya is a poor country, sometimes defined as less economically developed. It struggles to cope with rapid population growth.
- The Masai are a distinctive ethnic group in Kenya who are nomadic pastoralists. In 2009 there were over 800 000 Masai in Kenya. The Masai move their herds of cattle around the Kenyan savannah and steppe in search of water and grazing.
- The largest city in Kenya, and the capital, is Nairobi, with a population of 3.1 million. Kenya's second largest city is Mombasa, population 1.2 million.
- Kenya was a colony of the British Empire from 1888 to 1963 when it gained independence under the leadership of President Jomo Kenyatta.
- Brooke Bond has been growing and selling tea in Kenya since the 1920s. It is now owned by Unilever, and produces 32 million kg of tea a year.
- Kenya exports 35 000 tonnes of flowers to Europe each year. Kenyan flowers are sold by the main British supermarkets.
- In 2010 1.5 million tourists visited Kenya. Most tourists come to Kenya to go on safari to view the wildlife in the national parks and to enjoy the coral reefs and tropical beaches on the east coast near Mombasa.
- Tourism accounts for 22% of Kenya's export earnings (money that comes in to Kenya from other countries) and tourism employs 800 000 people. In 2012 nearly 200 000 tourists from the UK visited Kenya.

Masai

 Key Point

Kenya's main exports are tea (18%), flowers (10%) and coffee (5%), which are grown in the Kenyan Highlands.

Development Indicators for Kenya	
Gross Domestic Product (GDP) (per capita)	$1800
Employment Structure: Primary Secondary & Tertiary	75% 25%
Birth Rate (per 1000) Death Rate (per 1000) Natural Increase (per 1000)	30.1 7.1 23.0
Life Expectancy	63.3 years
Adult Literacy	87.4%
Human Development Index (HDI)	0.519 (145th out of 187 countries)

Kenyan beach

Quick Test

1. How large is Kenya?
2. When does Kenya experience its highest temperatures?
3. What is the capital of Kenya?

Key Words

equator
tropical equatorial forest
savannah grasslands
montane forest
tectonic plate
nomadic pastoralists
colony

Africa and Asia Compared – South Korea

You must be able to:

- Describe and explain the physical and human geography of South Korea
- Understand the similarities, differences and links between South Korea and other places.

Physical Characteristics

- South Korea is in East Asia and is part of the Korean Peninsula extending south from China into the Pacific Ocean.
- The area of South Korea is 99 617 km², less than half the size of the UK.
- Most of South Korea is mountainous, only 30% of the land area is suitable for building and agriculture.
- South Korea's highest mountain is Hallasan, a 1950 m high extinct volcano on the island of Jeju in the Korea Strait between South Korea and Japan.
- South Korea has a temperate monsoon climate. Annual temperatures range from –7°C to 29°C. Average annual rainfall varies between 600 mm in the north and 1500 mm in the south.
- The longest river in South Korea is the Nakdong (521 km).
- Most of South Korea's forests have been cut down. There is some tropical forest on the south coast of South Korea. Patches of deciduous and coniferous forest can be found throughout South Korea containing oak, birch, spruce and yew trees.
- South Korea is affected by tropical typhoons. In 2012 Typhoon Bolaveen struck the country with 186km/h (116mph) winds.

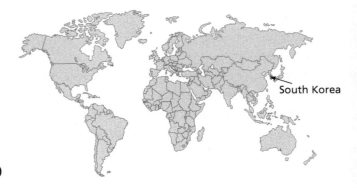

South Korea

Human Characteristics

- The population of South Korea was 48 million in 2013.
- The capital of South Korea is Seoul, its largest city, with a population of 10.3 million.
- South Korea is a developed country with the twelfth largest economy in the world, and is the world's sixth largest exporter.
- South Korea is home to global electronics and vehicle manufacturers including Samsung, LG, Daewoo, Hyundai and Kia (these large companies are known as chaebols).
- In 1945 Korea was liberated from Japan, which had ruled the country as a colonial power, by Soviet forces in the north and American forces in the south and the country was divided in two.

Key Point

19 people were killed by typhoon Bolaveen, 1.9 million homes lost power and damage costing $374.3 million was caused.

Traditional house

Seoul

- In 1950 a civil war began when North Korea invaded South Korea. A ceasefire was declared in 1953 after three million deaths; the contested border between the two had barely moved at all.
- In 1953 South Korea was an extremely poor country with a **gross domestic product (GDP) per capita** of $872 (in the UK the GDP per capita in 1953 was $11 972, in Kenya it was $339).
- In 1953 General Park Chung Hee took over the government and made changes that brought about rapid economic growth:
  - New roads were built to open up the country.
  - The government took over control of factories.
  - The government concentrated on the manufacturing industry including shipbuilding, vehicle manufacture, textiles and electronics.
  - New schools were built.
- In 1987 the first free elections were held. South Korea was the 18th largest economy in the world, 99% of people owned a television and most had fridges and washing machines.

Development Indicators for South Korea	
Gross Domestic Product (GDP) (per capita)	$33 200
Employment Structure: Primary Secondary Tertiary	6.9% 23.6% 69.4%
Birth Rate (per 1000) Death Rate (per 1000) Natural Increase (per 1000)	8.3 6.5 1.8
Life Expectancy	79.6 years
Adult Literacy	97.9%
Human Development Index (HDI)	0.909 (12th out of 187 countries)

Seoul

Geological Timescale 1

You must be able to:

- Explain what the Geological Timescale is and how it is constructed
- Explain what fossils are and why they are important
- Understand how living things have evolved over time.

The Geological Timescale

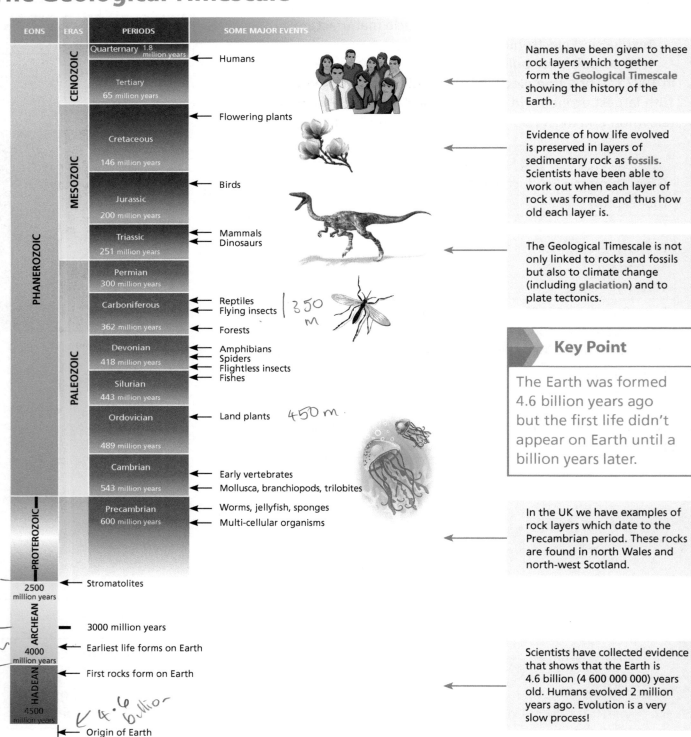

EONS	ERAS	PERIODS	SOME MAJOR EVENTS
PHANEROZOIC	CENOZOIC	Quarternary 1.8 million years	Humans
		Tertiary 65 million years	
	MESOZOIC	Cretaceous 146 million years	Flowering plants
		Jurassic 200 million years	Birds
		Triassic 251 million years	Mammals / Dinosaurs
	PALEOZOIC	Permian 300 million years	
		Carboniferous 362 million years	Reptiles / Flying insects / Forests
		Devonian 418 million years	Amphibians / Spiders / Flightless insects / Fishes
		Silurian 443 million years	
		Ordovician 489 million years	Land plants
		Cambrian 543 million years	Early vertebrates / Mollusca, branchiopods, trilobites
PROTEROZOIC		Precambrian 600 million years	Worms, jellyfish, sponges / Multi-cellular organisms
		2500 million years	Stromatolites
ARCHEAN		3000 million years	
		4000 million years	Earliest life forms on Earth
HADEAN		4500 million years	First rocks form on Earth / Origin of Earth

Handwritten annotations: 350 M; 450 m; 2.5; 3; 3.5; 4; 4.6 billion

Names have been given to these rock layers which together form the Geological Timescale showing the history of the Earth.

Evidence of how life evolved is preserved in layers of sedimentary rock as fossils. Scientists have been able to work out when each layer of rock was formed and thus how old each layer is.

The Geological Timescale is not only linked to rocks and fossils but also to climate change (including glaciation) and to plate tectonics.

Key Point

The Earth was formed 4.6 billion years ago but the first life didn't appear on Earth until a billion years later.

In the UK we have examples of rock layers which date to the Precambrian period. These rocks are found in north Wales and north-west Scotland.

Scientists have collected evidence that shows that the Earth is 4.6 billion (4 600 000 000) years old. Humans evolved 2 million years ago. Evolution is a very slow process!

The Fossil Record

- Present-day plants and animals are different to those that have been preserved as fossils. It wasn't until Charles Darwin wrote a book in the 19th century describing his theory of **evolution** that the fossil record was properly understood.
- Darwin said that, over time, living things change and develop new characteristics. Those creatures that are best adapted to their environment survive and those that are not, become **extinct**.
- When the Earth was first formed, there was no life. The first simple life forms were microscopic and lived in the sea. Eventually, around 450 million years ago, the first plants and animals colonised the land. Reptiles and flying insects appeared around 350 million years ago.

appeared after about 1 billion yrs; these life forms

- The dinosaurs were the dominant life forms on Earth for around 160 million years. Scientists believe they became extinct after an asteroid struck the Earth. Modern-day birds evolved from the dinosaurs.
- Humans have only lived on Earth for a very short period of time. If the entire Geological Timescale was reduced to a single day, humans would have been around for less than a minute:
  1. The Earth is formed at midnight.
  2. At 4.00 am the first simple life appears.
  3. At 10.46 pm the dinosaurs appear.
  4. At 11.58 and 43 seconds, the first humans appear!
- Humans are primates and descended from apes. Humans belong to a group of apes called 'hominids'.
  - The first humans appeared around 2.3 million years ago in Africa. These early humans learnt to use fire and simple tools. They survived by hunting and gathering wild food.
  - Modern-day humans are called Homo sapiens and have much larger brains than their early ancestors.
- Scientists have studied the evolution of humans from the remains of skeletons, particularly skulls, preserved in the soil. Using modern technology, they can work out what humans looked like in the past.

> **Key Point**
>
> Life on Earth evolves very slowly and humans have only appeared on Earth in very recent times.

Quick Test

1. How old is the Earth?
2. Who first wrote about the theory of evolution?
3. Where would you find the oldest rocks in the UK?
4. For how long did dinosaurs live on Earth?

> **Key Words**
>
> Geological Timescale
> fossils
> glaciation
> evolution
> extinct

Geological Timescale 2

You must be able to:

- Understand that the climate of the Earth has changed over millions of years
- Describe the effects of these climate changes
- Understand how the continents have changed position due to plate tectonics.

Changing Climates

- The climate of the Earth has changed many times in the past. Indeed when the Earth was first formed, it had no atmosphere. The young Earth would have been very hot with no water.
- Several times in the Earth's history the planet has become cooler. This has resulted in ice spreading from the polar regions across the land and oceans. These are called ice ages and the process of glaciation has helped to shape the surface of the Earth.
- The most recent ice age only finished about 10 000 years ago. This has happened at least five times before.
- During an ice age, the climate alternates between extreme cold for thousands of years (a glacial period) and then much warmer conditions (an inter-glacial period).
- In the last 100 years, humans have released a great deal of air pollution from factories and transport. These greenhouse gases trap heat in the atmosphere and cause the average temperature of the Earth to increase. This is global warming.
- Some people believe that the last ice age has not yet ended and that in fact average temperatures will in the future get very cold again.
- Glaciation is important because it affects sea level. When a lot of water is trapped on the land as ice, the sea level falls. When the ice melts, the sea level rises again.
- If all the ice at the polar regions melted, sea level would be much higher than at present and large areas would be flooded. This has happened many times in the geologic past.
- About 100 million years ago, during the Cretaceous period, much of the UK was under a warm tropical sea and the remains of small marine animals settled on the sea floor to form chalk.
- Over time, the rocks have been squeezed upwards and sea level has fallen. The chalk and the fossils formed in it can now be seen in the hills and cliffs of south-east England.

Key Point

The global climate has changed many times in the past. During glacial periods it has been much colder.

Key Point

During the last glaciation early humans moved south to escape the cold weather and animals such as the woolly mammoth became specially adapted to living in freezing conditions.

Moving Plates

- The Earth's crust is divided into many different sections called tectonic plates. These plates move a few centimetres per year. Although this seems very little, over millions of years it means the plates move hundreds, even thousands, of kilometres.
- The same fossils are found in Africa and South America. How is this possible? The answer is that millions of years ago, these two continents were joined together but have since slowly moved apart.
- Cynognathus was a large Triassic reptile, three metres long. Its remains have been found in both central Africa and central South America in sedimentary rocks that were formed around 250 million years ago. This happened when all the land masses formed a single continent called Pangaea (see p. 20).
- During the Permian period, around 300 million years ago, the UK was located much further south. Being closer to the equator, it had a desert climate. Evidence of this is found in red sandstone rocks that cover a large part of central England (Cheshire, Shropshire and Yorkshire).

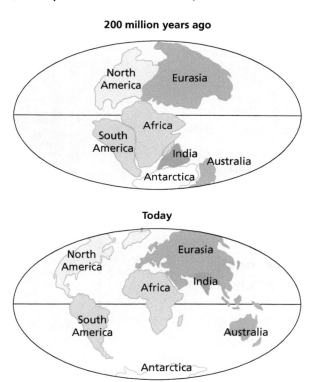

200 million years ago

Today

(see p. 20)

Key Point

The plates that form the Earth's crust move around very slowly and the continents that we know today were not always in the positions they are now.

Quick Test

1. What was the atmosphere of the Earth like when the Earth was first formed?
2. Why was the woolly mammoth woolly?
3. Where does air pollution come from?
4. How fast do the Earth's plates move?

Key Words

ice age
glacial period
inter-glacial period
global warming
sea level

Plate Tectonics 1

You must be able to:

- Understand the structure of the Earth
- Describe the different plate boundaries
- Understand the effects of plate movements.

Structure of the Earth

- The Earth is a rocky planet that formed billions of years ago.
- At the centre of the Earth is a hot but solid metal core. The core gives out heat that passes through the Earth. Around the core is a thick layer of semi-molten rock called the mantle. The hot rocks in the mantle are able to slowly flow.
- Around the outside of the Earth is a thin, solid layer called the crust. The crust is broken into a large number of separate sections called plates.
  - The plates that form the oceanic crust are relatively thin, with oceans such as the Atlantic lying on top.
  - The plates that form the continental crust are much thicker and form the main land masses such as Europe.
- Where two plates meet is called a plate boundary.
- The plates are constantly moving and changing position; for example, the plate that carries the UK was once much further south and the UK then had a desert climate.
- Many millions of years ago, all the continents were joined together in a single super-continent known as Pangaea. This super-continent split up into different sections as the crustal plates moved and this created the modern-day continents.
- Movement is still happening and each year the UK, on the Eurasian Plate, gets further away from the USA, which lies on the North American Plate.

Plate Boundaries

- There are three types of plate boundary and the movement of the plates is different at each one.
- Movement along the plate boundaries causes earthquakes and volcanoes.

> ### Key Point
>
> The Earth's crust is broken into sections called plates. These plates move very slowly in different directions.

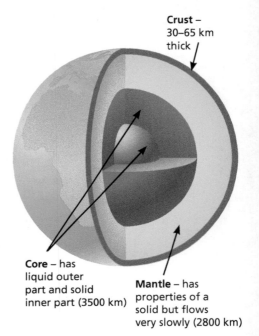

Crust –
30–65 km
thick

Core – has
liquid outer
part and solid
inner part (3500 km)

Mantle – has
properties of a
solid but flows
very slowly (2800 km)

Tectonic plates

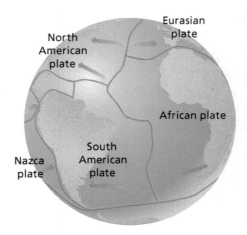

Eurasian plate

North American plate

African plate

Nazca plate

South American plate

At a **destructive plate boundary**, the plates are moving towards each other. The plates get squeezed together and sometimes one plate disappears beneath the other and is slowly destroyed.

The squeezing of the rocks due to great heat and pressure causes the land to rise and mountains to form. The Himalayas in Asia are still rising due to these powerful forces.

At a **constructive plate boundary**, the plates are moving away from each other. Molten magma rises up through the gaps created by this process, cools, hardens and forms new land.

Most constructive plate boundaries occur under the oceans and this creates underwater volcanoes which may form volcanic islands such as Iceland.

In East Africa, the Great Rift Valley is one of the few examples of a constructive plate boundary on land. This part of Africa is splitting in two. Where Arabia has split from the rest of Africa, water has filled the crack to form the Red Sea.

At a **conservative plate boundary**, land is neither being created nor destroyed as two plates are simply sliding past each other. The main consequence of this is earthquakes, some of which may have disastrous results.

The most famous conservative plate boundary is the San Andreas Fault in California, USA. In 1906, a devastating earthquake flattened San Francisco destroying over half the homes and killing around 3000 people.

Key Words

core
mantle
crust
plate
plate boundary
destructive boundary
constructive boundary
conservative boundary

Quick Test

1. Which layer in the Earth is hottest?
2. What are the sections of the crust called?
3. In which continent are the Andes?
4. In what year was most of San Francisco destroyed by an earthquake?

Plate Tectonics 2

You must be able to:

- Understand what an earthquake is and why they happen
- Understand what a volcano is and why they erupt
- Know what dangers are caused by these two natural disasters.

Earthquakes

- An earthquake is a violent shaking of part of the Earth's crust. Thousands of tiny earthquakes happen every day.
- Earthquakes are caused by a sudden movement of the rocks along a plate boundary. The most damaging earthquakes happen along destructive and conservative plate boundaries.
- This sudden movement sends out shockwaves, which quickly travel through the rocks of the crust.
  - The point at which the shockwaves start, usually deep underground is called the focus of the earthquake.
  - The point at which the shockwaves reach the surface and cause damage is called the epicentre.
- Shockwaves slowly lose their power as they move through the rocks so the most damage is done at the epicentre and damage decreases as you move away from this point.
- If an earthquake occurs under the ocean, the movement of the sea bed may cause a powerful wave called a tsunami.
- In 2004 a tsunami in the Indian Ocean killed almost a quarter of a million people and affected 14 different countries. With waves up to 30 m (100 ft) high, it was one of the deadliest natural disasters in recorded history.

The Aftermath of Earthquakes

- As the ground shakes during an earthquake, it may crack. This causes damage to buildings, roads, railways and bridges. Underground pipes and cables can be broken leading to gas escaping and fires breaking out.
- After an earthquake, thousands of people may be left homeless without easy access to shelter, food or clean water. As a result, many people may die in the weeks after the earthquake.
- Vital buildings such as hospitals, schools and police stations may also be destroyed.
- International aid may be sent from other countries to help the victims of the earthquake. This can include tents, bottled water and food.
- Experts with special equipment and sniffer dogs may also be sent to help search for people trapped in the wreckage.

Key Point

Earthquakes can cause death and destruction but fortunately these are rare. Earthquakes are most common along the edges of the plates.

Volcanoes

- A **volcano** is a mountain formed from molten rock ejected from a hole in the Earth's crust. It can build up over hundreds of years.
- Volcanoes occur on land and under the sea.
- Volcanoes are formed along the edges of constructive and destructive plate boundaries. A line of volcanoes is found along the west coast of the USA where the Pacific Plate meets the North American Plate, for example.
- A few volcanoes are also created in other areas called hot spots. These are weaknesses in the Earth's crust where molten magma can escape to the surface and cool as lava.
- A volcano will consist of either lava on its own or alternating layers of lava and ash.
  - If the lava is very runny, the volcano will be very wide but not very tall. These are shield volcanoes. The volcanoes in Hawaii are this shape.
  - If the lava is thick and sticky, it can form tall, narrow volcanoes. These are composite volcanoes. Mount St Helens (USA), Mount Fuji (Japan) and Mount Etna (Italy) are this shape.

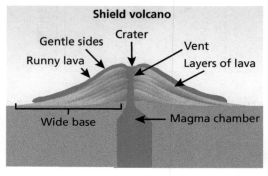

Shield volcano — Gentle sides, Crater, Vent, Runny lava, Layers of lava, Wide base, Magma chamber

Composite volcano — Ash, Thick, sticky lava, Crater, Secondary cone, Steep sides, Vent, Layers of ash and lava, Narrow base, Magma chamber

- People like to live near volcanoes because the land can be fertile and good for growing crops.
- If the volcano erupts, people may have to be evacuated to a safe place. Hot lava or ash can damage buildings and kill or injure people.
- Eventually, most volcanoes become **dormant** and stop erupting.

 Key Point

Volcanoes can bring benefits to humans but they are also dangerous when they erupt.

Key Words

earthquake
focus
epicentre
tsunami
volcano
dormant

Quick Test

1. How common are tiny earthquakes?
2. What is the focus of an earthquake?
3. Why are fires common after an earthquake?
4. What is lava?

Key Concepts from Key Stage 2

World Geography

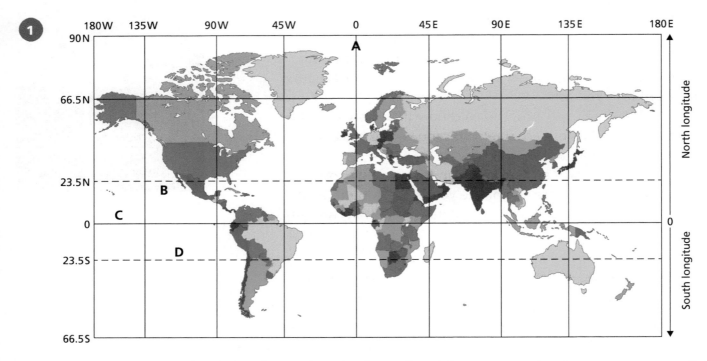

a) Complete the table below by writing the letter from the map next to the correct name of the line in the table.

Equator	
Tropic of Capricorn	
Tropic of Cancer	
Greenwich Meridian	

[4]

b) Which colour are the following countries on the world map?

i) Brazil   **ii)** Argentina   **iii)** Italy   **iv)** USA   **v)** Sweden   [5]

Physical Geography

2 **a)** **i)** Name the scale that is used to measure the magnitude of an earthquake. [1]

ii) What is the word for the point on the ground surface above where an earthquake happens? [1]

iii) What is the word for a volcano that is never going to erupt again? [1]

b) i) Write the labels in the correct places on the diagram.

Tributary   **Confluence**   **Watershed**   **Mouth**   **Source**

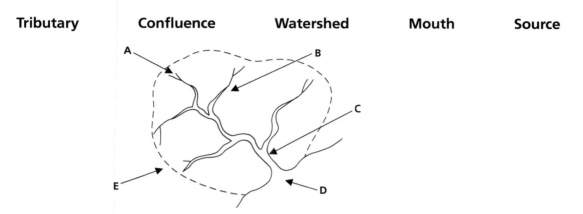

[5]

ii) Describe how the water cycle works by using the words below to fill in the gaps.

groundwater   **evaporation**   **run-off**   **precipitation**   **condensation**

The sun heats the sea which causes _____. Water vapour rises into the sky

and as it cools _____ takes place to form clouds. The water droplets fall as

rain, snow or hail, also known as _____. The water flows back to the sea in

streams and rivers as _____ and through soil as _____ .   [5]

Human Geography

3 **a)** Match each type of economic activity with the correct occupation.

Primary Activity		Dentist

Secondary Activity		Farmer

Tertiary Activity		Metal Worker

[3]

b) Choose the correct settlement types from the pair of choices in the sentences below.

i) Most **towns/cities** in the UK have a cathedral, hospital and university.   [1]

ii) A **village/hamlet** is a rural settlement with a small population that is unlikely to
    have a church or primary school.   [1]

iii) A region where a number of urban areas have grown together is known as a
    city/conurbation.   [1]

Practice Questions

Location Knowledge – Russia, China, India and the Middle East

1 **a)** Why does the majority of Russia's agriculture take place in the steppe regions? [2]

   b) Underline the correct words in the following sentences.

     In Russia's semi-arid regions, temperatures can reach **50°C / 80°C / 100°C**. Rainfall is less than **250 mm / 500 mm / 750 mm** per year. [2]

2 **a) i)** What is the capital city of Russia? [1]

     ii) What is its population? [1]

   b) Suggest two reasons why Russia's population is declining. [4]

3 Why do you think China's economy has grown so quickly in the last 30 years? Tick (✓) the correct answers.

People can own and run their own businesses ☐

People are spending less ☐

The government has encouraged international trade ☐

People don't like to work hard ☐ [2]

4 Why is the Indo-Gangetic plain in India so good for agriculture? [3]

5 **a)** Give reasons for India's rapid population growth. [3]

   b) Why are so many Indians living on $1.25 a day when India has the third largest economy in the world? [2]

6 Why was Jawaharlal Nehru important in India's history? [4]

7 **a)** How much land area does the Middle East cover? [1]

   b) Which three continents have countries that are part of the Middle East? Tick (✓) the correct options.

Europe	☐	North America	☐
South America	☐	Africa	☐
Asia	☐	Australasia	☐

[3]

8 Why is the Suez Canal such an important waterway? [3]

Africa and Asia Compared – Kenya and South Korea

1 **a)** Where is the Rift Valley in Kenya? [1]

b) How was the Rift Valley formed? [3]

2 Which of the following are Kenya's three main exports?
Tick (✓) the correct answers.

Rice	☐	Coffee	☐	
Tea	☐	Cocoa	☐	
Cotton	☐	Flowers	☐	[3]

3 Why is the rate of population growth in Kenya a problem for the country? [3]

4 **a)** Fill in the gaps in the following sentences:

In 2012, _____ tourists from the UK visited Kenya. They come

to Kenya mainly to go on _____ and to visit the beaches near

Kenya's second largest city, _____. [3]

b) Why is tourism so important to Kenya? [3]

5 What is meant by the term 'chaebol'? [2]

6 **a)** Give the methods used by the South Korean government to achieve rapid
economic growth. [6]

b) How did South Korea's GDP change between 1953 and 1987? [2]

7 Tick (✓) the boxes next to the statements which are true.

South Korea's longest river is the Nakdong River ☐

South Korea's capital city is Nairobi ☐

A free trade agreement exists between the EU and South Korea ☐ [2]

8 **a)** When did Typhoon Bolaveen hit South Korea? [1]

b) What impact did the typhoon have on the country? [3]

Geological Timescale

1 **a)** What is the Geological Timescale? [2]

   b) How long after the Earth was formed did the first life forms appear? [1]

   c) What is a fossil? [2]

2 Which group of animals did birds evolve from?

Tick (✓) the correct option.

Reptiles ☐

Dinosaurs ☐

Early vertebrates ☐

Molluscs ☐ [1]

3 What are hominids? [1]

4 Why did it not rain when the Earth was first formed? [1]

5 **a)** How did humans survive the very cold weather during the last glaciation? [2]

   b) During a glaciation, what happens to sea-level and why? [2]

6 What effect do greenhouse gases have on the Earth's climate?

Tick (✓) the correct options.

Greenhouse gases allow heat out of the atmosphere ☐

Greenhouse gases trap heat in the atmosphere ☐

The climate becomes warmer ☐

The climate becomes cooler ☐ [2]

Plate Tectonics

1 **a)** Label the diagram of the Earth.

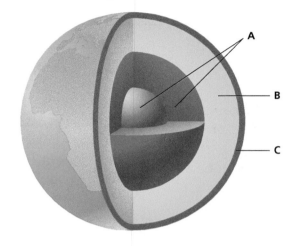

[3]

b) Why is the crust often described as being as thin as an eggshell? [1]

c) What effect does the heat from the core have on the mantle layer? [2]

2 What name is given to the ancient super-continent before it broke up into
the modern-day continents? [1]

3 **a)** What is an earthquake? [1]

b) What happens at the epicentre of an earthquake and why? [2]

4 Why did the 2004 Indian Ocean tsunami kill so many people? [2]

5 What is international aid? Give an example. [2]

6 Tick (✓) the statements that are true.

All volcanoes are made of lava and ash ☐

Volcanoes in Hawaii are low and wide ☐

A dormant volcano is one which has recently erupted ☐

Land near volcanoes is fertile ☐ [2]

Rocks and Geology 1

You must be able to:

- Understand the difference between porous and non-porous rocks
- Identify the three types of rock: sedimentary, igneous and metamorphic
- Understand how the different types of rock form.

What are Rocks?

- All rocks are made up of grains and every grain is a **mineral**.
- The grains in the rock can be different shapes, sizes and colours, and how they fit together decides whether it will be a hard or soft rock.
- **Porous** rocks with round grains have spaces or gaps. Water gets into them and the rock is often soft and crumbly.
- **Non-porous** rocks have tightly fitting grains and water cannot get in.

Types of Rock

- **Sedimentary** rocks are formed from deposits originally eroded from older rocks and living organisms:
  1. Rocks (igneous, metamorphic or other sedimentary rocks) are weakened by weathering and worn away by erosion.
  2. Worn away material is transported as fragments or dissolved in water and carried by ice, gravity, wind, sea and rivers.
  3. Transported material is eventually deposited (laid down) in shallow seas, lakes or hollows in the landscape. These deposits form beds of sediment (layers).
  4. Some beds might be the remains of living things. For example, coal beds are formed from the remains of ancient plants.
  5. Beds of sediment are compacted (pressed and squeezed together) as the weight of sediment increases. In the end all the loose sediment is stratified (layered) and cemented (joined) into solid rock (**lithified**).
  6. Remember: there are pores (spaces) between the sediments. This weakens the rock, so sedimentary rocks are said to be soft.
- This process can take millions of years.
- Examples include chalk, limestone, sandstone, shale, clay, coal, conglomerate and breccia.
- **Igneous** rocks are formed when magma cools and solidifies:
  1. The inside of the Earth is very hot – hot enough to melt rocks. Molten rock is called magma.
  2. Magma tends to rise upwards in the Earth's crust. If it spills out on to the surface it is called lava.
  3. As magma cools it forms igneous rocks.

Key Point

To name a rock and understand how it is formed a geologist asks: 'What minerals does it contain, and how are the minerals held together?'

Key Point

Sedimentary rock makes up 7% of the Earth's crust.

Carboniferous sandstone
The sandy grains in this rock leave spaces between one another. It is soft, crumbly and porous. This specimen formed during the Carboniferous period 299 to 358 million years ago and shows a fossilised fish.

Key Point

Igneous rock makes up 65% of the Earth's crust.

4 As magma cools its mineral crystals begin to grow.

5 The slower the magma cools the bigger the crystals.

6 Igneous rocks are hard and **crystalline**. There are no obvious pores in igneous rocks.

- Examples include granite, gabbro, basalt, pumice, obsidian and volcanic ash.
- **Metamorphic** rocks are formed when heat and/or pressure cause rocks to change without melting.

  1 Movements in the Earth can cause rocks to be deeply buried, squashing them or moving them closer to molten magma.

  2 Heat and pressure cause the chemical elements in the original rock to react and re-form into new minerals.

  3 As metamorphism occurs, no elements are taken and none added; they are simply rearranged.

  4 Remember that metamorphic rocks do not form from melted rock – melting causes igneous rocks to form.

  5 The new minerals in metamorphic rocks have crystals that are arranged in layers.

  6 Metamorphic rocks can be formed from sedimentary or igneous rocks.
- Examples include marble, slate, schist and gneiss.

Rock types in Earth's crust

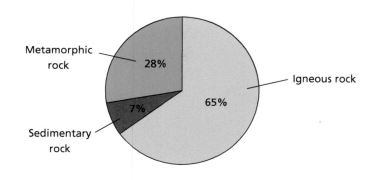

Metamorphic rock 28%

Igneous rock 65%

Sedimentary rock 7%

Key Point

Extrusive igneous rocks have cooled quickly outside the earth. **Intrusive** igneous rocks have cooled slowly inside the earth.

Granite
The grains fit tightly together in this rock so it is hard and non-porous. This rock formed between 354 and 417 million years ago.

Key Point

Metamorphic rock makes up 28% of the Earth's crust.

Key Words

mineral
porous
non-porous
sedimentary
lithified
igneous
crystalline
extrusive
intrusive
metamorphic

Quick Test

1. Which type of rock tends to be softer – porous or non-porous?
2. Rearrange these terms into the correct order so they show the processes by which sedimentary rocks form: lithification / transportation / erosion / deposition.
3. What is molten rock called?
4. Which type of rock forms from molten rock?

Rocks and Geology 2

You must be able to:

- Explain the rock cycle
- Understand how weathering and erosion affect rocks.

The Rock Cycle

- The rocks that make up the Earth are recycled and do not stay the same forever.
- Igneous rocks are formed from magma from the mantle.
- Metamorphic and sedimentary rocks use 'second-hand' materials.
- Sedimentary rocks are formed from other rock types that have been broken down by weathering and erosion.
- Metamorphic rocks are rocks that have been changed by heat and pressure.

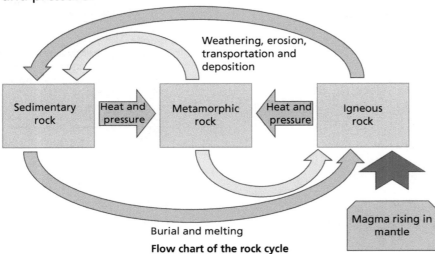

Flow chart of the rock cycle

Cross-section of the rock cycle

Key Point

Think about the effect that rocks have on the UK landscape. The highest areas, igneous and metamorphic, are found in the west and north-west of the UK and the sedimentary rocks are found in the south and south-east.

Weathering and Erosion

- All rocks gradually wear away. *by the action of weather, plants and animals.* This is called **weathering**.
- Weathering involves the interactions of many things, for example, rainfall, temperature and atmospheric gases.
- Weathering produces rock, mineral and chemical debris where the original rock was exposed.
- Material produced from weathering is transported by gravity, rivers, sea, ice and wind, before being deposited as sediment.
- The agents of transportation move sediment and also produce more of it. This process is called **erosion**.

> **Key Point**
>
> Erosion uses a transport agent to remove material and take it elsewhere. Weathering breaks down rock into fragments – no movement is involved.

Physical Weathering

- Mainly occurs because of the effects of changes in temperature. The presence of water can assist the process.
- The two main types of physical weathering are: freeze-thaw (water freezing in cracks expands and breaks rocks apart) and exfoliation (also known as 'onion-skin weathering'; cracks develop parallel to the land surface as pressure is released, or fast temperature change causes expansion and contraction).

Chemical Weathering

- Occurs as rainwater reacts with minerals to form new minerals. Rainwater is slightly acidic. Higher temperatures aid the process of chemical weathering.
- There are three different types of chemical weathering:
  - Solution – the removal of rock in solution by acidic rainwater.
  - Hydrolysis – acidic water producing clay and salts.
  - Oxidation – rocks broken down by oxygen and water.

Biological Weathering

- Trees put roots through joints and cracks in the rock; the roots eventually break the rocks open.
- Some animals, like limpets, scrape and dissolve rock away.
- Bacteria and lichens break down the rocks on which they live.

Quick Test

1. Name three things that interact to cause weathering.
2. What happens to water to make it split rocks open?
3. What two substances break down rocks during oxidation?
4. How do trees break open rocks?

> **Key Words**
>
> weathering
> erosion

Weathering and Soil 1

You must be able to:

- Describe weathering
- Explain the four main processes of weathering: chemical, freeze-thaw, onion-skin and biological weathering.

Weathering

- Weathering is the breakdown of rocks by the action of the weather, plants and animals.
- **Chemical weathering** takes place when weak acid in rainwater dissolves rocks:
  1. Limestone is made from a mineral called calcium carbonate.
  2. This reacts with weak carbonic acid in rainwater to form soluble minerals.
  3. These are washed away and the limestone is weathered.

Carbonation

1 Rainwater

Cloud

Acid rain

2 Crack

3 Cracks enlarged as rock is weathered

- **Freeze-thaw weathering** happens in cold, usually mountainous, locations:
  1. Water gets into cracks in rocks.
  2. The water freezes and expands.
  3. This puts pressure on the rock causing it to split and break up.

Freeze–thaw

1 10°C

Water

Crack

2 −5°C

Ice expands

Pressure

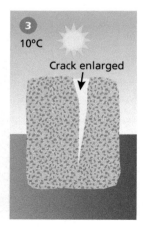
3 10°C

Crack enlarged

- **Onion-skin weathering** occurs in places where there is a significant difference between day and night temperatures, such as in deserts:
  1. During the day the sun heats the rocks causing them to expand.
  2. During the night the rocks cool down and contract.
  3. The surface of the rocks heats up and cools down faster than the core of the rocks which creates stress and tension in the rock.
  4. Eventually the surface layers of the rock crack and begin to peel away like the outer layers of an onion.

Expansion   Contraction   Rock fractures

Onion-skin weathering (exfoliation)

- **Biological weathering** occurs when rocks are broken down by plants and animals.
  1. Plant roots are able to force their way through weaknesses in rocks.
  2. As the plants grow the roots widen and the rocks are cracked and split apart.
  3. Burrowing animals may also break up rocks as they dig through the ground.

Biological weathering

Quick Test

1. What is weathering?
2. What does the weather have to be like for onion-skin weathering to take place?

Key Words

chemical weathering
freeze-thaw weathering
onion-skin weathering
biological weathering

Weathering and Soil 1: Revise   35

Weathering and Soil 2

You must be able to:

- Understand how soil is formed
- Describe the structure of soil including the different layers
- Compare soil in the UK with soil in tropical rainforests.

Soil

- Soil is the upper layer of the Earth's surface where plants grow.
- Soil is formed from a mixture of weathered rock and decayed plant and animal matter known as humus. Most soils also contain billions of micro-organisms, insects, worms, water and air.
- The factors that influence the formation of soil are:
  - Climate – high temperatures increase the rate of soil formation.
  - Organisms – micro-organisms, insects, worms and plants.
  - Parent material – the type of rock that the soil has been weathered from.
  - Relief – the shape of the land.
  - Time.
- Approximately 75 billion tonnes of soil are lost from fields due to soil erosion globally each year, which is equivalent to 100 000 km^2 of farmland disappearing.
- It can take hundreds of years for 1 cm of soil to form so many people consider soil to be a non-renewable resource.

> **Key Point**
>
> The formation of soil is affected by climate, organisms, parent material, land relief and time.

Soil Structure

- Soil can be divided up into several distinct layers or horizons.
  - The O horizon is the surface layer consisting of fallen leaves and twigs, animal droppings and dead creatures.
  - The A horizon, or topsoil, is the layer of soil directly beneath the surface; it is rich in nutrients, minerals and humus.
  - The B horizon, or subsoil, is where the weathered parent rock is becoming soil and nutrients from the topsoil are leached downwards by rainwater.
  - The C horizon is the rock or parent material, that the soil has been formed from.
  - The R horizon is the solid bedrock at the base of the soil.

Soil structure

Soil in the UK

- The soil found in deciduous woods and forests in the UK is known as brown earth; it covers 45% of the UK.
- Brown earth is usually 1–2 m deep with a relatively thick layer of topsoil (20 cm on average).
- Brown earth soil is approximately 10 000 years old.

Brown earth

Topsoil

> ### Key Point
>
> Soil is essential for life to survive on the planet. Without soil plants could not grow, animals would have nothing to eat and ultimately humans would not be able to feed themselves.

Soil in Tropical Rainforests

- The soil found in tropical rainforests is known as latosol. It has formed over 100 million years and can be 20–30 m deep.
- The topsoil is thin (2–5 cm deep) due to the rapid recycling of nutrients from dead plants and creatures by the forest and the leaching of nutrients by heavy rainfall.

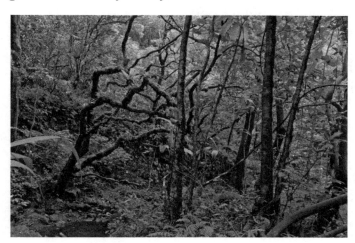

> ### Quick Test
>
> 1. What is the word for decayed plant and animal matter found in soil?
> 2. What does topsoil contain?
> 3. How deep can soils in tropical rainforests become?

> ### Key Words
>
> humus
> parent material
> non-renewable
> horizons
> topsoil
> subsoil
> bedrock
> brown earth
> latosol
> leaching

Weather and Climate 1

You must be able to:

- Outline the different elements that make up the weather
- Understand how weather is recorded
- Understand why weather changes over time.

What is Weather?

- **Weather** is the daily changes in the atmosphere that affect, and sometimes control, human activity.
- Weather elements include:
  - temperature
  - precipitation
  - wind
  - humidity
  - air pressure.
- **Temperature** tells us how hot or cold the air is at a particular time. Humans are interested in the minimum (lowest) temperature, the maximum (highest) temperature and the temperature range (the difference between maximum and minimum).
- **Precipitation** is the rainfall, sleet, snow and hail that reaches the ground.
  - Hail is formed from ice pellets and snow from ice crystals.
  - Sleet is partly melted snow.
- Wind direction affects the temperature of the air. In the UK, winds which come from the north bring cold air and winds blowing from the south bring warmer air. High wind speeds can cause damage to trees and property.
- **Humidity** is the amount of moisture in the air. On damp, foggy days there will be lots of moisture in the air; on hot, sunny days the air may be quite dry.
- **Air pressure** is an important weather element. When warm air rises, the air pressure is reduced and when cold air sinks, the air pressure is increased.

Measuring Weather

- In order to make a weather forecast, it is important to collect weather data that shows what is happening now.
- Most modern weather instruments are electronic and connected to computers that record and analyse the measurements they make.
- A rain gauge is used to record rainfall, which is measured in millimetres. In south-east England, about 600 mm of rainfall is recorded each year but in the north-west, the figure may be as high as 3000 mm per year.

> **Key Point**
>
> Weather is the daily changes in the atmosphere.

> **Key Point**
>
> The movement of air from areas of high pressure to areas of low pressure causes the wind.

- A thermometer is used to record temperature. Temperature is recorded using degrees Celsius (°C) or degrees Fahrenheit (°F). The UK has distinct seasons with colder temperatures in winter (average around 5°C) and hotter temperatures in summer (average around 17°C).
- Wind speed is recorded with an instrument called an anemometer. The units may be mph, m/s or knots.
- Wind direction is recorded with a wind vane that uses compass directions or degrees.
- Air pressure is recorded with a barometer. The units of pressure are called millibars (mbs).
- A weather station may also record the amount and type of clouds in the sky.
- Satellite images can show us detailed pictures of cloud cover over very large areas. Many weather satellites are also fitted with rainfall radar that shows where it is raining.

 Key Point

Weather data needs to be collected regularly in order to create a weather forecast.

Weather Forecast

- A daily weather forecast helps us to make decisions about what to wear, what we might eat and where we might go.
- Farmers need forecasts to plan when to sow seeds or harvest crops, and airlines and rail companies need to plan for bad weather.
- A weather forecast for the next 24 hours can be very accurate. It can tell us what the temperature is likely to be, what the risk of rain is and when the rain may arrive at a particular place. It can also predict frost, fog and high winds that may cause problems for people.
- As computers have become more powerful, we are also now able to predict the weather up to a month in advance. These forecasts, however, are not as accurate.

Why Does the Weather Change?

- The air in our atmosphere is constantly on the move. This is caused by heating from the sun.
- Once air is warmed, it becomes lighter and rises (think of a hot air balloon). Rising air will eventually cool again, causing clouds to form. These may produce rain or snow.
- Places near the sea normally get much wetter weather as the wind picks up moisture from the sea and carries it over the land.

 Key Point

Solar energy is strongest near the equator and weakest near the north and south poles.

 Key Words

weather
minimum temperature
maximum temperature
temperature range
precipitation
humidity
air pressure

Quick Test

1. What is weather?
2. What is another name for rainfall?
3. What does an anemometer measure?

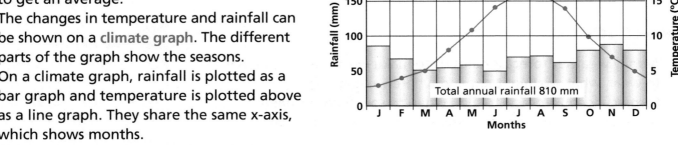

Weather and Climate 2

You must be able to:

- Recognise what a climate graph looks like and how it is constructed
- Understand the differences between the main climate zones which cover the Earth
- Understand why climate varies from place to place.

What is Climate?

- **Climate** is the pattern of average temperature and rainfall data over a year. Data is collected for a minimum of 30 years to get an average.
- The changes in temperature and rainfall can be shown on a **climate graph**. The different parts of the graph show the seasons.
- On a climate graph, rainfall is plotted as a bar graph and temperature is plotted above as a line graph. They share the same x-axis, which shows months.
- A climate graph can be used to calculate:
  - maximum temperature
  - minimum temperature
  - temperature range
  - wettest month
  - driest month
  - total annual rainfall.

Range of temperature: 13°C

Total annual rainfall 810 mm

Types of Climate

- The world is covered by different **climate zones**. These are large areas that share the same pattern of temperature and rainfall.
- The UK, and many parts of Western Europe, has a **temperate climate** of warm summers, mild winters and a high total rainfall.
- In North Africa and the Middle East there is a **desert climate**. *(arid)* This is very hot all year round and has a low total rainfall.
- In the northern part of South America, central Africa and South East Asia, there is a **tropical climate**. This is hot all year round with a high total rainfall.
- In the Arctic and Antarctica, there is a **polar climate**. This has very low temperatures and a low total rainfall. Most precipitation falls as snow.

include
Medit.

Key Point

Climate is the seasonal changes in temperature and rainfall over a year.

Factors Affecting Climate

- The climate zones stretch around the world in bands parallel to the lines of latitude. As you travel north from the equator, you will pass through tropical, then desert, then temperate and finally through polar climate zones.

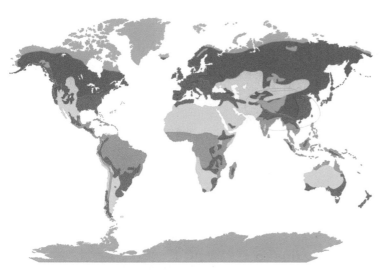

Key:
- ■ Temperate climate
- ■ Desert climate
- ■ Tropical climate
- ■ Polar climate

- In general, it gets colder as you move from the equator to the poles. This is because the energy from the sun is strongest at the equator and weakest at the poles.
- In equatorial areas (between the Tropic of Cancer and the Tropic of Capricorn) the sun is always overhead for part of the year and its energy passes through less of the atmosphere.
- In polar areas, the sun's energy strikes the Earth at a low angle and so passes through a thicker layer of atmosphere. Some energy is lost by reflection back into space.
- **Altitude** (height above sea level) also affects climate. In mountain areas it is almost always colder, with more rain and snow falling each year when compared with lowland areas.
- The location of a place affects climate since places near the sea are generally milder and wetter than places which are in the middle of the large continents.
  - In the middle of Russia, it is very hot in summer and very cold in winter.
  - In the UK, which is the same distance from the equator, it is warm in summer and mild in winter.
- Warm and cold **ocean currents** will also affect places near the coast. The warm waters of the Gulf Stream flow from the Gulf of Mexico towards the UK and make our climate much milder than it would be otherwise in winter.
- The cold waters of the Labrador Current flow south from Greenland towards Canada and make the climate of the entire coast of Canada much colder.
- In California an offshore cold current causes thick, cold fogs to form along the coast, while inland temperatures may reach 30°C.

Quick Test

1. What two things are shown on a climate graph?
2. Where might we find a tropical climate?
3. What kind of climate do most Middle East countries have?
4. What does the word altitude mean?

Key Words

climate
climate graph
climate zone
temperate climate
desert climate
tropical climate
polar climate
altitude
ocean current

Glaciation 1

You must be able to:

- Describe what a glacier is and where they are found
- Understand how glaciers form
- Describe how glaciers shape the landscape
- Recognise erosional landforms created by glaciers.

What and Where are Glaciers?

- A glacier is a large moving body of ice that flows slowly due to the force of gravity.
- Ice in the form of glaciers, ice sheets and ice caps covers 10% of the Earth's land area.
- Glaciers can be found at high altitudes in mountain ranges or in the far north and south latitudes of the Arctic and Antarctica where temperatures are low enough for them to form.

How a Glacier Forms

- Glaciers form where more snow falls each year than can melt; the resulting build up of snow is called accumulation.
- Over time, the weight of the accumulated snow causes the layers beneath to become compacted and dense. At this stage it is called firn.
- The process of glacier ice formation is very slow and takes hundreds of years.
- The weight of the ice mass causes it to slide and advance downhill due to gravity.
- In warmer months melting, or ablation, may take place at the snout of the glacier causing it to retreat.

Key Point

20 000 years ago ice covered most of the UK during the glacial period known as the Pleistocene.

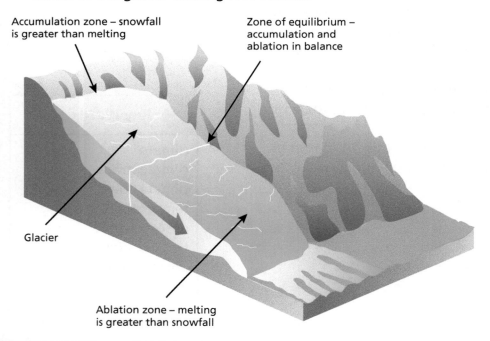

Accumulation zone – snowfall is greater than melting

Zone of equilibrium – accumulation and ablation in balance

Glacier

Ablation zone – melting is greater than snowfall

- Processes of weathering and erosion carve out the landscape:
  - **Freeze-thaw**: when water freezes and expands in cracks in rock causing it to break apart.
  - **Plucking**: when melt water at the base and sides of a glacier freezes around rocks, which are then plucked from the landscape as the glacier advances.
  - **Abrasion**: when rocks carried along by the glacier scour and smooth the landscape.

Erosional Landforms

- Corries are hollow-shaped landforms.
  1. After the glacial ice has melted a lake may remain in the corrie. This is known as a tarn (for example, Red Tarn in the Lake District).
  2. Aretes are a knife-like ridge that form when two corries are back to back (for example, Striding Edge in the Lake District).
  3. Pyramidal peaks form when three or more corries form back to back (for example, Stob Dearg in Scotland).
  4. U-shaped valleys are created as the glacier advances. It will widen, deepen and straighten the valley from a V shape to a U shape.
  5. Ribbon lakes are long, narrow lakes that can be found in U-shaped valleys when less resistant rock on the valley floor is eroded more deeply by the glacier (for example, Lake Windermere in the Lake District).
  6. Hanging valleys and waterfalls can be found at the sides of this U-shaped valley. They show how smaller valleys entering the main valley have been cut off by the wide and deep glacier.
  7. Truncated spurs are the cut-off (truncated) hills that once led towards the main valley.

Revise

Key Point

Erosional landforms seen across the UK provide evidence of the past glacial age.

Corrie formation

Key Words

accumulation
firn
ablation
snout
retreat
freeze-thaw
plucking
abrasion

Quick Test

1. Name the two main processes of glacial erosion.
2. Explain the formation of glacial firn.
3. Describe the shape of a corrie.
4. Describe and explain the formation of a hanging valley.

Glaciation 2

You must be able to:

- Describe and explain the formation of depositional landforms
- Explore the problems of managing glacial landscapes
- Define sustainable tourism.

Depositional Landforms

- **Moraine** is the name given to the material deposited after the glacier melts.
  - Terminal moraine marks the farthest advance of the glacier.
  - Lateral moraine is deposited along the sides of the glacier.
  - Medial moraine forms where the lateral moraine of two glaciers running side by side is deposited as a ridge along the centre of a valley after melting.
- **Drumlins** are hills shaped like half-buried eggs or teardrops. They are pointed in the direction that the glacier advances. They are often found in groups known as 'a basket of eggs'.
- Drumlins are formed in this way:
  1. Glacier meets obstruction on valley floor.
  2. Moraine is deposited behind the obstruction.
  3. Glacier moves over obstruction and streamlines it.
  4. The downstream end is tapered by the advancing glacier.
- **Erratics** are large rocks or boulders that may have been transported hundreds of kilometres by a glacier and deposited when it melted.
- Erratics may be a completely different rock type to that found in the area where they are dropped.

> **Key Point**
>
> Drumlins are typically 1–2 km long, less than 50 m in height and around 500 m wide.

Direction of glacier flow

100 m

Drumlin

1.5 km

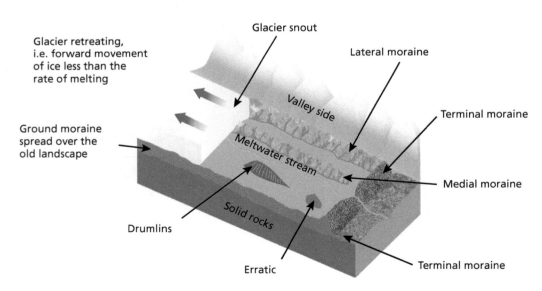

Glacier retreating, i.e. forward movement of ice less than the rate of melting

Glacier snout

Lateral moraine

Valley side

Terminal moraine

Ground moraine spread over the old landscape

Meltwater stream

Medial moraine

Solid rocks

Drumlins

Erratic

Terminal moraine

Managing Glacial Landscapes

- Glacial landscapes are often beautiful areas with dramatic scenery and landforms that attract many tourists.
- An area that attracts large numbers of tourists is known as a honeypot site.
- Glacial landscapes are also home to local people who work, farm or may have retired there.
- Environmentalists and conservationists will be involved in protecting these unique areas.
- If tourism is to be sustainable then the impacts on local people, the economy and the environment need to be managed in a balanced way.

Conflict in Glacial Landscapes

- Conflict may arise due to the different demands of farmers, environmentalists and tourists and needs careful management by local councils.
- Visitor centres are a good way to begin educating tourists on how to protect these unique landscapes.

Tourist Impact	Problem	Solution
Footpaths overused	Vegetation destroyed, land eroded	Divert popular routes to allow old paths time to recover
Speedboats	Noise and water pollution, erosion	Speed limits Promote sailing
Dog walkers	Disturb sheep	Keep dogs on leads in farm areas
Traffic	Traffic jams	Promote public transport and bike paths

> **Key Point**
>
> Sustainable tourism is tourism that is managed to ensure future generations can continue to enjoy these unique landscapes.

Quick Test

1. Describe the shape of a drumlin.
2. Why do erratics have a different rock type to the area in which they are found?
3. Explain two ways in which tourist activities might cause problems for local people in a honeypot area.

Key Words

moraine
drumlin
erratic
honeypot
sustainable

Review Questions

Location knowledge – Russia, China, India and the Middle East

1 How cold can it get in the tundra regions of the far north of Russia? [1]

2 **a)** Define the term 'natural resource'. [2]

    b) Give three examples of high-tech industries found in Russia. [3]

3 What is the capital of China and how many people live there? [2]

4 **a)** When was the Sichuan earthquake? [2]

    b) How large was the earthquake on the Richter scale? [1]

    c) How many people died in the Sichuan earthquake? [1]

5 What is the land area of the Indo-Gangetic plain? [1]

6 Which is the largest religious group in India? Tick (✓) the correct option.

Sikh	☐	Hindu	☐	
Christian	☐	Muslim	☐	
Jew	☐	Buddhist	☐	[1]

7 Name four of India's main industries. [4]

8 **a)** Name two deserts that are found in the Middle East. [2]

    b) How large is the Rub' al Khali and how high can its sand dunes reach? [2]

9 Which of the following are oil-exporting countries in the Middle East? Tick (✓) the correct options.

Qatar	☐	Bahrain	☐	
Turkey	☐	Kuwait	☐	
Israel	☐	Oman	☐	[4]

Africa and Asia Compared – Kenya and South Korea

1 How many times larger is Kenya than the UK? [1]

2 What is Kenya's total annual rainfall and how does this compare to the UK's rainfall? [2]

3 The photo shows montane forest in Kenya. Define the term 'montane forest'. [2]

4 Name South Korea's highest mountain and give its height. [2]

5 Name three types of trees that are found both in the UK and South Korea. [3]

6 What is the life expectancy in South Korea? [1]

7 **a)** When did South Korea achieve independence and from which country? [2]

b) How many people were killed during the civil war between North and South Korea? [1]

Geological Timescale

1. The picture shows a fossil. Which rock type contains fossils? [1]

2. a) What name is given to the oldest rocks in the UK? [1]

   b) Where in the UK are these rocks found? [1]

3. What does the theory of evolution say about which creatures survive over geologic time? [2]

4. Why did the dinosaurs become extinct? [2]

5. a) Where in the world did the first humans appear? Tick (✓) the correct option.

   Europe ☐

   Antarctica ☐

   Africa ☐

   Asia ☐ [1]

   b) What are Homo sapiens? [1]

   c) What is different about the brains of modern humans compared to their ancestors? [1]

6. Why is it possible that the Earth could get colder rather than warmer in future? [2]

7. a) How were the chalk rocks found in south-east England formed? [2]

   b) Why are there ancient desert rocks in central England? [2]

Plate Tectonics

1 **a)** What is a plate boundary? [1]

b) Name a large mountain range formed at a plate boundary. [1]

c) When two plates move apart at a constructive plate boundary, what fills the gap that is created? [2]

2 Explain why the UK is getting further away from the USA each year. [2]

3 **a)** What is a tsunami? How are they linked to earthquakes? [3]

b) During an earthquake, the ground shakes and cracks. What problems does this cause? [2]

c) Why do many people die in the weeks after an earthquake? [2]

4 What is a hot spot? [2]

5 The photo shows Mount St Helens, a volcano on the west coast of the USA.

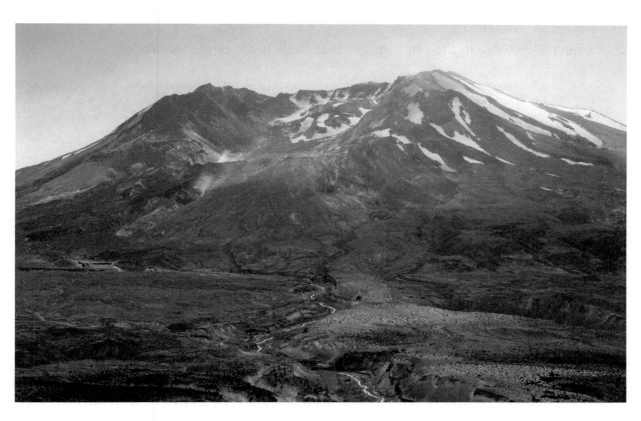

a) Why is there a line of volcanoes along the west coast of the USA? [2]

b) Explain why people might want to live near a volcano. [2]

Rocks and Geology

1. **a)** How are igneous rocks formed? [2]

   b) Why do some igneous rocks have bigger crystals than others? [4]

2. **a)** What percentage of the Earth's crust is made from metamorphic rocks? [1]

   b) Match up the following sedimentary rocks with the metamorphic rocks that they turn into.

Sedimentary	Metamorphic
Limestone	Slate
Shale	Marble

   [2]

3. Why are some types of rock more likely to contain fossils than others? [2]

4. Study the photograph of the chalk cliffs below. Chalk is a sedimentary rock formed from the shells and skeletons of dead sea creatures.

   What evidence is there in the photograph that chalk is a sedimentary rock? [2]

Weathering and Soil

1 **a)** Name an environment where freeze-thaw weathering is likely to take place. [1]

b) Number these sentences 1–3 to explain how onion-skin weathering takes place.

A During the night rocks cool down and contract. ☐

B The surface layers of rock crack and peel away. ☐

C During the day rocks heat up and expand. ☐ [3]

2 Describe how plants and animals can cause rocks to break up. [2]

3 **a)** Match up the factors that affect the formation of soil with their definitions.

Factors	Definitions
Climate	the type of rock that the soil has weathered from
Organisms	the shape of the land
Parent material	high temperatures increase the rate of soil formation
Relief	insects, worms and plants

[4]

b) Which factor is missing from the list in question 3a)? [1]

4 How much soil is lost each year from fields due to soil erosion?

Tick (✓) the correct option.

10 billion tonnes ☐

50 billion tonnes ☐

75 billion tonnes ☐

100 billion tonnes ☐ [1]

5 What is the name given to the soil found in tropical rainforests? [1]

Weather and Climate

1. Weather includes temperature, precipitation and air pressure, and which two other elements? [2]

2. Draw lines to match each weather aspect with what it measures.

Minimum temperature	Amount of moisture in the air
Humidity	Amount of moisture that reaches the ground
Precipitation	Lowest temperature recorded each day

[3]

3. What is hail? [1]

4. When air sinks, will this increase or decrease air pressure? [1]

5. What sort of workers might use a weather forecast? Explain how it helps them. [2]

6. When air is warmed by the sun, what happens to it? [1]

7. Label the two weather elements on the climate graph. [2]

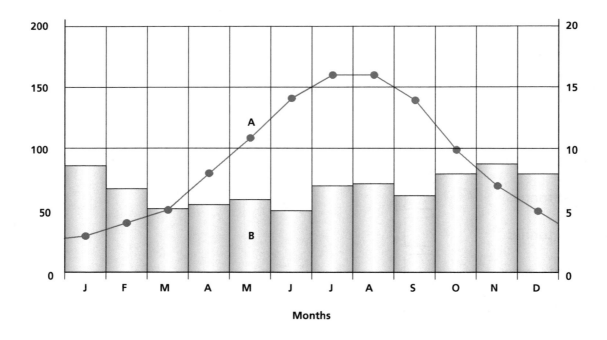

8. Where would you find an equatorial area? [2]

9. What is the Gulf Stream? [3]

Glaciation

1 **a)** Define a glacier. [2]

b) What was the Pleistocene? [1]

c) Describe how glaciers are formed including the following key terms: [5]

Accumulation   **Compacted**   **Firn**   **Advance**   **Gravity**

2 Name the three main processes of glacial weathering and erosion. [3]

3 Name the three types of moraine labeled below:

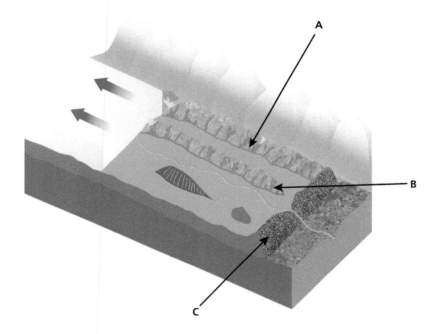

[3]

4 Fill in the missing words from the description of drumlin formation.

a) Glacier meets _____ on valley floor.

b) Moraine is _____ behind the obstruction.

c) Glacier moves over obstruction and _____ it.

d) The downstream end is tapered by the _____ glacier. [4]

5 Explain three ways in which tourism can have a negative impact on glacial landscapes. [6]

Rivers and Coasts 1

You must be able to:

- Explain key processes and landforms
- Describe the features found along the river's course
- Understand how people interact with these environments.

Rivers

- Rivers flow from source to mouth, passing through three main stages: upper, middle and lower.
- Main features at each stage:

Stage	Dominant Processes	Landforms
Upper	Erosion	V-shaped valley, rapids, waterfalls, gorges
Middle	Erosion and deposition	Meanders, ox-bow lakes
Lower	Deposition	Floodplains and levees

Key Point

These main processes will work together to form specific landforms.

- Three main processes take place in rivers and coastal zones.
  1. **Erosion** is a high energy process in which material is worn away.
  2. **Transportation** is the process by which eroded material is carried away.
  3. **Deposition** is a low energy process in which transported material is deposited.

River

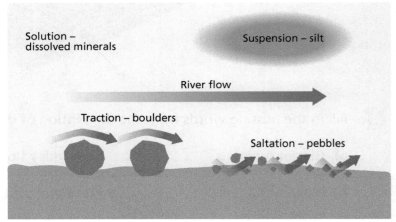

Transportation

Erosional Processes

- The key erosional processes are:
  1. **Corrasion** (or abrasion) is the erosion of river beds and banks by rocks carried with the water.
  2. **Attrition** is the process by which rocks become smaller and rounder over time as they repeatedly crash into each other.

③ Slightly acidic water can erode some types of rock in river beds and banks by dissolving in a solution.

④ Hydraulic action is the erosion of river beds and banks owing to the sheer force of water power.

Landform Formation

- **Waterfalls** – formed through vertical erosion of alternating bands of resistant and less resistant rock; undercutting; plunge pool formation; the waterfall retreats and a steep gorge forms.
- **Meanders** – lateral erosion on outside bend, with deposition on inside bend; bend increases in sinuosity over time.
- **Floodplains** and **levees** – caused by deposition during river floods; the coarsest material builds up on banks to form levees. Finer silts are deposited from the channel onto floodplains.

Flooding

- A river will flood when water flows into the channel faster than it can be carried downstream. It will overflow its banks and spread out on to the surrounding floodplains.
- Rivers can be managed to try and create a long-term solution to flooding impacts:
  - **Hard engineering** involves using artificial materials to alter the natural flow of the river.
  - **Soft engineering** involves using natural measures to reduce flood risk, e.g. afforestation.
- Physical and human factors contribute to flooding:

Physical	Human
Heavy rain	Urbanisation
Steep slopes	Deforestation
Impermeable rock	
Many tributaries	
Saturated soil	

> **Key Point**
>
> Soft engineering is viewed as a more sustainable approach to river management.

> **Key Point**
>
> All of these factors will cause rainwater to flow overland to the river channel. This is the quickest route for water to reach the channel.

> **Key Words**
>
> erosion
> transportation
> deposition
> waterfall
> meander
> floodplain
> levee
> hard engineering
> soft engineering

> **Quick Test**
>
> 1. What are the four processes of erosion at work in a river?
> 2. What is deposition?
> 3. Which process must be present for the formation of floodplains and levees?

Rivers and Coasts 2

You must be able to:

- Describe the formation of waves
- Explain the formation of coastal landforms
- Consider approaches to coastal management.

Coasts

- Coasts are the narrow zone between the sea and the land.
- Coastal zones are under constant attack from waves and weather.
- Rates of weathering and erosion will vary depending on the rock type of the coast.
- Differential erosion creates distinct landforms and discordant coastlines with bays and headlands.
- Characteristics of discordant coastlines are:

Headlands	Bays
Hard rock, e.g. chalk	Soft rock, e.g. clay
Waves hit headland with force	Waves refracted into bays
Caves, arches, stacks, stumps	Beaches

Wave Formation

- Wind blowing over the surface of the sea transfers energy to the water by friction.
- This energy transfer sets up a circular motion in the water, like rollers on a conveyor belt.
- Wave energy is transferred forward in the direction of the prevailing wind – the water itself does not move forward.
- As a wave reaches the shore the bottom of the 'roller' meets the sea floor. Friction between the water and the sea floor causes the wave height to increase.
- The top of the wave moves faster than the bottom and the wave topples over as a breaker.

Erosional and Depositional Landforms

- Caves, arches, stacks and stumps are formed in the following way:
  1. Destructive waves attack the exposed headland.
  2. Weaknesses in the headland become cracks and in time caves are formed.
  3. Continued erosion from beneath and weathering from above creates an arch.
  4. The roof of the arch collapses to leave a stack.
  5. The stack decreases in size into a stump.

Key Point

Energy within a wave is transferred forward.

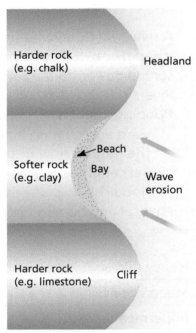

**Discordant Coastline —
Bays and Headlands**

Backwash more powerful than swash

Weak swash

Destructive waves

Swash more powerful than backwash

Constructive waves

- Wave-cut platforms are formed in this way:
  1. At high tide waves attack the base of the cliff.
  2. A **wave-cut notch** forms.
  3. Weathering from above causes the unsupported cliff to collapse.
  4. The sea removes collapsed material.
  5. The process repeats, and the cliff retreats.
  6. A smooth **wave-cut platform** is revealed at low tide.
- Once eroded, material is transported along the coastline in the direction of the prevailing wind via the zig-zag movement of **longshore drift**.
- Sand is carried up the beach at an angle (swash) and returns down the beach in a straight line (backwash).

Wave-cut platform

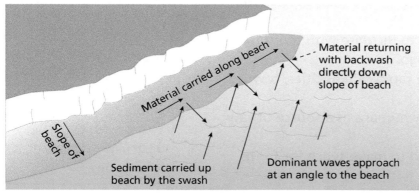

Longshore drift

How People Manage Coasts

- Decisions about how to manage the coast can lead to conflict between people with different interests. Residents, tourists, environmentalists, local and national government may all have opposing views.
- A number of hard and soft engineering strategies may be used in an attempt to reduce the impact of destructive waves and the loss of sand via longshore drift.

Hard Engineering	Soft Engineering
Curved sea wall – deflects destructive waves	Beach nourishment – ensures wide beach
Rock armour – breaks up wave energy	Managed retreat – coast left to retreat
Groynes – slow longshore drift	
Offshore reef – waves break offshore	

Key Words

differential erosion
discordant
weathering
arch
stack
stump
wave-cut notch
wave-cut platform
longshore drift

Quick Test

1. Which two elements will lead to coastal erosion?
2. Where do waves get their energy from?
3. What is the process by which sand is transported along the coast?
4. Which group of people may prefer soft engineering approaches?

Landscapes 1

You must be able to:

- Consider the ways in which people interact with natural landscapes
- Understand how these interactions may contribute to climate change
- Understand how these interactions may contribute to desertification.

People and the Earth

- The world's population grew to over 7 billion in 2011.
- Human activities have had an impact on more than 80% of the Earth's land surface.
- The impact of human activity began to increase with the shift to agriculture around 10 000 years ago.
- The built landscape is increasing at a rapid rate as cities, towns and transport technologies grow.
- The natural landscape is exploited by humans as a source of raw materials and energy:
  - Trees and vegetation are removed to make space for farms and cities.
  - Mines and quarries are dug for natural resources.
  - Rivers are controlled to provide electricity.
  - Fumes and emissions from transport and factories have an impact on the atmosphere.
  - Oceans, rivers and lakes suffer from pollution and overfishing.
- As populations grow, so too does the demand for space and resources and more fragile landscapes are exploited.
- How humans use, modify and change landscapes may not be sustainable.

People and Rainforests

- Tropical rainforests cover less than 5% of the Earth's surface and play a vital role in the Earth's ecosystem.
- In 2013 there were an estimated 370 billion trees in the Amazon rainforest.
- There may be as many as 5 million species in the world's rainforests, of which only about 10% are known to science.
- As population grows the demand for wood, resources and land increases.
- This means that rainforests are being exploited and cleared resulting in deforestation.

- Deforestation results in erosion as soils are unprotected from rain.
- Nutrients are washed away and lost from the soil, resulting in loss of vegetation, leading to a decline in wildlife.

Deforestation and Climate Changes

- With fewer trees, less moisture is evaporated back into the atmosphere.
- This means less rainfall and more drought conditions.
- Trees act as 'carbon sinks', taking carbon dioxide out of the atmosphere.
- Burning the rainforests releases carbon dioxide into the atmosphere.
- Carbon dioxide is one of the greenhouse gases that contribute to global warming.

People and Savannah Grassland

- Savannah grasslands form on the fringes of rainforests and towards desert margins where there is insufficient rainfall to support forests.
- As population increases, people are exploiting these fragile landscapes.
- This leads to desertification as overgrazing by cattle and overcultivation results in soil erosion, leading to an increasing amount of land turning into desert.
- Desert environments are fragile with a low carrying capacity.
- Carrying capacity = the maximum number of people that the land can support.

Desertification

- Results from a combination of physical processes and human activity.
- Land becomes infertile and unproductive.
- It is a serious problem in the Sahel region of Africa where many countries meet the edges of the Sahara Desert.
- Affects some of the poorest people in the world.

 Key Point

Climate change is also responsible for increased dry periods and less rainfall.

 Quick Test

1. Why are fragile landscapes exploited?
2. Why are rainforests described as 'carbon sinks'?
3. Where do savannah grasslands form?
4. Define desertification.

 Key Words

natural resources
sustainable
deforestation
carbon sink
greenhouse gases
desertification
carrying capacity

Landscapes 2

You must be able to:

- Understand how indigenous people live in rainforests
- Consider how indigenous people are important in fragile landscapes
- Explore sustainable strategies to prevent soil erosion in savannah landscapes.

Indigenous People in Rainforests

- There are many indigenous people, such as the Yanomamo in the Amazon rainforest of Brazil, who have lived in the tropical rainforests for thousands of years.
- It is important to understand that indigenous people have much to teach us about rainforests.
- They are hunter-gatherers, finding food, clothing, and housing from the forest.
- Indigenous people move their villages regularly to allow the landscape to recover and grow back.
- They live a sustainable existence because they use the land without destroying the environment.
- Indigenous populations are decreasing because:
  - Their homes are being destroyed by deforestation.
  - They are killed by introduced diseases, such as measles, for which they have no resistance.
  - They are forced into cities by governments who claim to own their land.

Key Point

Humans have interacted with the landscape for thousands of years, but with an increasing population comes an increasing demand for resources and land. This can lead to the destruction of natural landscapes.

Working with Indigenous People

- By working with indigenous people we can learn important information about rainforests, such as their ecology, medicinal plants, food and other products.

Key Point

Indigenous people can be employed to educate investors about the environment.

- Indigenous people can teach valuable lessons about managing rainforests sustainably.
- It is crucial to realise that they have a right to practise their own lifestyle, and live upon the land where their ancestors have lived before them.

Sustainable Management

Rainforests

- **Reafforestation** by planting trees to replace the ones cut down.
- Conservation by creating protected areas of rainforest.
- **Agroforestry** by planting crops alongside trees rather than cutting them down.
- Satellite photography can be used to monitor illegal deforestation and disruption to indigenous people.

Savannah Grasslands

- Reduce grazing so plants have chance to grow again and so prevent soil erosion and desertification.
- Circles of stones ('magic stones') are placed on the ground to hold water on the soil and prevent run off.
- Planting trees provides shelter from the wind.
- Mulching by adding layers of leaves or straw can reduce evaporation and add nutrients to the soil.
- **Terracing** prevents soil from being washed down slopes when it rains.
- Drought-resistant plants can be used to stabilise the soil.

Terracing prevents soil from being washed down slopes

Quick Test

1. How do indigenous people survive in rainforests?
2. How can indigenous people help manage rainforests?
3. What is reafforestation?
4. What are 'magic stones'?

Population 1

You must be able to:

- Understand how world population is changing
- Understand where people live in the world
- Explain why some areas have many people and others have few.

World Population

- The world population has already passed 7 billion (7 000 000 000) people.
- About 130 million babies are born each year. The number of babies born per 1000 people per year is called the birth rate.
- About 50 million people die each year. The number of people dying per 1000 people per year is called the death rate.
- Over the last 1000 years, birth and death rates roughly balanced each other out and there was little population growth.
- Over the last 150 years, however, the rate of population growth has gradually increased – some people call this a 'population explosion'.
- Birth rates are now falling in most parts of the world and so the total world population may level out at around 10 billion people.

> ### Key Point
>
> Geographers and others are worried that there may not be sufficient resources (food, water, minerals, etc.) for the world's growing population.

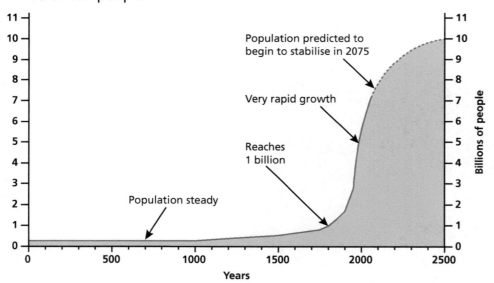

Population Distribution

- Population distribution means where people live.
- A sparse population (few people) occurs in areas where it is difficult to live (deserts, mountains, marshes and very cold environments).
- Areas with a sparse population include the Sahara Desert, the Himalayas and the Arctic.

[handwritten note: b/c the of a lack of natural res's]

- A **dense population** (lots of people) is found in areas where humans can locate most of the things they need (land suitable for building, fertile soil for farming, mineral resources and water).
- Areas with a dense population include most of Western Europe, the eastern USA and large parts of South East Asia.
- In some countries where there are valuable mineral resources, such as oil, people use their wealth and modern technology to create artificial environments. Examples include:
  - Alaska (very cold) in the USA
  - Dubai (very hot and dry) in the Middle East.

Population Density

- **Population density** is used to measure the number of people in an area (number of people per square kilometre, for example).
- Although population density is an average figure, it allows us to compare how crowded countries are. It is important to remember that even in crowded countries there may be areas with only a few people.
- One of the countries with the highest population density is Bangladesh where there are an average 988 people per square kilometre. This can be compared with South Korea (505), the UK (262), China (141), Egypt (85), Peru (24) and Russia (8).
- In the United Kingdom, the most crowded place is London with a population density of over 5000 people per square kilometre. The Highlands of Scotland by comparison has a population density of only 10 people per square kilometre.

> **Key Point**
>
> The number of people living in different parts of the world depends mainly on the climate (average temperature/rainfall) and the resources available.

People per km²
- ■ Above 50
- ■ 10 to 50
-    Fewer than 10

> **Quick Test**
>
> 1. Roughly how many 'extra people' are there in the world each year?
> 2. If the world population continues to grow, why may this be a problem in some areas?
> 3. Why do few people live in very cold or very dry areas?
> 4. Why is the population density in most of Europe very high?

> **Key Words**
>
> birth rate
> death rate
> population growth
> population distribution
> sparse population
> dense population
> population density

Population 2

You must be able to:
- Explain why people move
- Understand how and why population changes
- Know about population problems.

Population Migration

- When people move from one place to another, this is known as **migration**.
  - The people choosing to leave a country are known as **emigrants**.
  - The people arriving in a new country are called **immigrants**.
- There are laws controlling migration and if people enter a country without permission, they are referred to as illegal immigrants.
- The majority of people who move are economic migrants, seeking higher paid work and a better life.
- If people are forced to leave a country because of famine, war or a natural disaster, they become **refugees**. Many countries such as the UK have special agreements to help refugees start a new life.

Key Point

The number of people living in a country can change naturally or through migration or a combination of the two.

Population Change

- If there are more births than deaths in a country, there will be a natural population increase.
- If there are more immigrants than emigrants, there will be a population increase due to migration.
- In the Low Income Countries (LICs) there have been, until recently, very high rates of natural population increase. As the birth rates fall, however, they begin to match the death rates more closely and population growth slows down.
- In the High Income Countries (HICs) birth and death rates are roughly the same so there is little natural population change each year.

Population change

Country	Continent	Birth Rate	Death Rate
Denmark	Europe	10.3	10.2
United Kingdom	Europe	12.3	9.3
India	Asia	20.9	7.5
Saudi Arabia	Middle East	21.1	3.3
Ethiopia	Africa	42.9	11.1

- Birth rates may be high for many different reasons, including:
  - religious beliefs
  - a lack of contraception
  - in the poorest countries many infants die before they are a year old so people have large numbers of children to compensate.
- In some countries, the government may try to persuade people to have fewer babies through **family planning** campaigns.
- In the poorest countries, high death rates are caused by **poverty**, a lack of food, disease and poor medical care.
- In the richest countries, death rates may still be high due to lack of exercise and poor diet leading to high rates of obesity, cancer and heart disease.

Population Issues

- A rapidly growing population may mean a country doesn't have sufficient resources to provide for the needs of all the people. The **quality of life** for the majority of people may then be low. A few African countries are still in this difficult situation.
- An ageing population (many people over the age of 60 years) is a problem for some of the HICs. A good quality of life and good medical care mean that large numbers of people are living longer.
- An **ageing population** may not have enough people of **working age** to do all the jobs and the older people may need lots of special help and care, which can be very expensive.
- Countries that receive large numbers of refugees fleeing from war and disasters may struggle to provide food, shelter and medical care.
- In the 28 countries of the European Union, people are allowed to migrate freely from one country to another. Many people migrate from the poorer countries of Eastern Europe (Romania, Bulgaria) to the richer countries of Western Europe (Germany, UK) where there are better paid jobs – this can cause unrest.

Refugee camp

> ### Quick Test
>
> 1. What is the difference between emigrants and immigrants?
> 2. Why do refugees need help?
> 3. Calculate the difference between birth and death rates for the UK and for India.
> 4. Why are death rates still high in countries such as the USA and the UK?

Urbanisation 1

You must be able to:

- Define urbanisation
- Explain the causes of urbanisation
- Understand the characteristics and effects of urbanisation in the UK.

What is Urbanisation?

- **Urbanisation** is the process by which the proportion of people living in urban areas grows. This will happen when more people move to live and work in towns and cities than remain in the countryside.
- **High Income Countries (HICs)**, such as the UK, USA and Germany, have experienced urbanisation since the 19th century and are now considered to be urbanised.
- **Low Income Countries (LICs)**, such as Nigeria and Kenya, are experiencing rapid urbanisation today.

Causes of Urbanisation

- Causes of urbanisation include:
  - **Rural to urban migration:** the movement of people from countryside (rural) to towns and cities (urban).
  - **Natural increase:** number of births is greater than number of deaths.

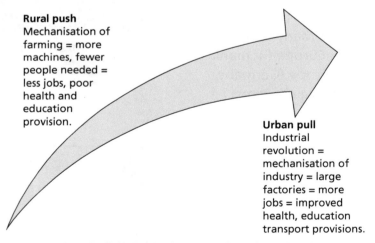

Rural push
Mechanisation of farming = more machines, fewer people needed = less jobs, poor health and education provision.

Urban pull
Industrial revolution = mechanisation of industry = large factories = more jobs = improved health, education transport provisions.

Push and pull factors leading to rural to urban migration

Experience of Urbanisation in HICs

- During the Industrial Revolution (18th to early 20th century) UK cities grew as manufacturing industries provided jobs and opportunities.

- The proportion of the UK population living in urban areas grew steadily:
  - 1700 – 17%
  - 1800 – 26%
  - 1900 – 77%
  - Today – 90%
- **Suburbanisation** took place from the 1950s onwards as cities spread and grew outwards.
- Pollution and overcrowding in city centres meant people wanted to live further away.
- Improvements in technology, such as transport infrastructure, increased car ownership and telecommunications meant people could commute more easily or even work away from the urban centre.
- **Counterurbanisation** took place from the 1980s onwards as people moved even further away from major urban areas to smaller towns and villages.

Effects of Recent Urban Processes in HICs

- Increase in population and employment away from city centres.
- Large shopping centres attract people from suburbs and beyond.
- Inner cities suffer from derelict factories, abandoned shops, poor quality housing, unemployment, crime, poor environment.
- **Urban decline** became a problem across the UK. For example, the decline of the London Docklands from the 1950s as large container ships could no longer access the port resulted in rising unemployment, poverty and poor quality housing.

Response to Urban Decline in the UK

- **Urban regeneration** projects were initiated in many UK cities in an attempt to attract people and businesses back to the cities.
- The London Docklands Development Corporation was set up in 1981 to attract new businesses, money and people to the area.
  - Abandoned warehouses were converted into flats and apartments.
  - The Docklands Light Railway improved links to the rest of London.
  - The Millennium Dome (now the O2 Arena) was built to provide entertainment and leisure attractions.
  - A shopping centre was built close to Canary Wharf.

Quick Test

1. Define urbanisation.
2. Explain how push and pull factors lead to urbanisation.
3. Explain how suburbanisation comes about.
4. Why did UK cities need regeneration projects?

Key Words

urbanisation
high income countries (HICs)
low income countries (LICs)
rural to urban migration
suburbanisation
counterurbanisation
urban decline
urban regeneration

Urbanisation 1: Revise   67

Revise

Urbanisation 2

You must be able to:

- Understand the characteristics and effects of urbanisation in LICs
- Recognise the difference between HICs' and LICs' experience of urbanisation
- Explain the importance of sustainable urban management.

Experience of Urbanisation in LICs

- Lower income countries (LICs) have experienced rapid growth of urban populations since the 1950s; for example in China the urban population grew from 13% in 1950 to 52.6% in 2012.
- A **megacity** is defined as a city with a population greater than 10 million. By 2025 it is estimated that there will be 29 megacities in LICs globally.
- LIC cities struggle to provide housing, services and jobs to meet the needs of their expanding populations.
- New arrivals are forced to live in makeshift housing on unwanted land around the city.
- These slum areas are known as **'shanty towns'** ('favelas' in Brazil, 'bustees' in India).
- Despite the poor living conditions, they are often described as hopeful and active places where everything is recycled imaginatively. Dharavi, a large slum in Mumbai, India, has over 300 000 'rag-pickers' who collect and recycle 80 per cent of Mumbai's waste.
- Local communities, charities and governments are working to help improve the quality of living in shanty towns.

> ### Key Point
>
> Unlike the steady growth of HIC cities over 200 years, LIC cities have grown rapidly in just 60 years, making it difficult for governments to provide sufficient homes and services.

Effects of rapid urbanisation in LICs – shanty towns

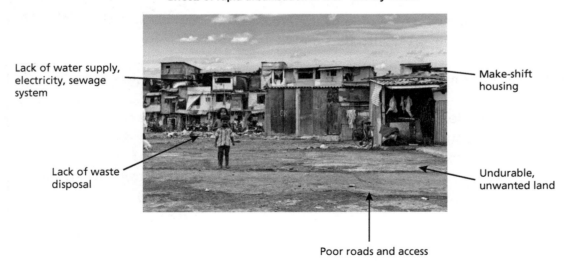

Lack of water supply, electricity, sewage system

Make-shift housing

Lack of waste disposal

Undurable, unwanted land

Poor roads and access

- The grassroots approach involves the shanty town inhabitants in the planning process and has proved to be very successful.
- **Self-help schemes** give local people ownership of their land and provide them with training and tools to improve their homes themselves.

Sustainable Urban Management

- Many people are working towards trying to make cities more sustainable.
- A **sustainable city** offers a good quality of life to current residents but doesn't reduce the opportunities for future residents.
- Society (people), the economy (money) and the environment must all be considered equally in the planning process. People must have equal access to jobs and facilities within the city on affordable public transport, which will ease traffic congestion and pollution.

A sustainable city

Energy efficient homes (i.e. with solar panels/well insulated)

Open green spaces

Street lighting makes cities safer

Recycling bins

Traffic calming in roads

Walking and cycling is safe – pedestrianised streets

Bus and bike lanes

> **Quick Test**
>
> 1. What is the major difference between the experience of urbanisation for HICs and LICs?
> 2. Describe a 'shanty town'.
> 3. What is meant by the term 'grassroots approach'?
> 4. What three things must be considered if a city is to be managed sustainably?

> **Key Words**
>
> **megacity**
> **shanty town**
> **self-help scheme**
> **sustainable city**

Rocks and Geology

1 Define the term 'porous rock'. [1]

2 **a)** **i)** What are sedimentary rocks made from? [2]

ii) Name three sedimentary rocks. [3]

b) **i)** Which two processes are required for metamorphic rocks to form? [2]

ii) Name three metamorphic rocks. [3]

3 What is the difference between intrusive and extrusive rocks? [2]

4 Study the diagram of the formation of sedimentary rocks. Match the processes from the list below with the correct places on the diagram.

Processes

Particles build up in layers. _____

Over millions of years new rock forms on the sea bed. _____

Particles sink to the bottom of the sea. _____

Eroded particles transported by rivers to the sea. _____

[4]

5 Study the photograph of Hay Tor in Dartmoor in the UK. Hay Tor is made from granite, which is an igneous rock.

Explain how igneous rocks are formed.

[4]

Weathering and Soil

1 Name the mineral in limestone and the acid in rainwater that react together during chemical weathering. [2]

2 Number these statements **1–3** to explain the process of freeze-thaw weathering.

Water freezes and expands. ☐

Water gets into cracks in rocks. ☐

Rocks split and break up. ☐ [3]

3 Why does repeated heating and cooling cause the surface of rocks to split and flake off when onion skin weathering takes place? [4]

4 What is the difference between weathering and erosion? [2]

5 **a)** How much soil is lost from fields worldwide each year due to soil erosion? [1]

b) Why do some people describe soil as a non-renewable resource? [1]

c) Describe three factors that affect the rate of soil erosion. [3]

6 Describe three characteristics of brown earth. [3]

7 **a)** How much of the UK is covered by brown earth? Tick (✓) the correct answer.

10% ☐

25% ☐

45% ☐

65% ☐ [1]

b) How old is brown earth soil? Tick (✓) the correct answer.

1000 years ☐

10 000 years ☐

100 000 years ☐

1 million years ☐ [1]

Weather and Climate

1 Which of the following are types of solid precipitation?

Tick (✓) the correct options.

Hail ☐

Rain ☐

Snow ☐ [2]

2 **a)** Why is it important to know the direction that the wind is blowing from? [1]

b) Why do people worry about high wind speeds in the weather forecast? [1]

3 If a rain gauge measured a total rainfall for the year of about 600 mm, in which part of the UK would it be most likely to be located?

Tick (✓) the correct option.

North-west England ☐

South-east England ☐ [1]

4 On a foggy day, is humidity likely to be high or low? [1]

5 Which will be more accurate and why?

Tick (✓) the correct option, then give your reason.

A weather forecast for the next 24 hours ☐

A weather forecast for the next 30 days ☐ [2]

6 In the UK, how much hotter is it in summer than in winter? [3]

7 **a)** Put the following climate zones in the correct order as you travel from the North Pole to the equator:

desert climate   **temperate climate**   **polar climate**   **tropical climate** [4]

b) What sort of temperature and rainfall pattern would be found in a tropical climate? [2]

8 Why is some of the sun's energy lost by reflection near the North and South Poles? [2]

Glaciation

1 What does accumulation mean? [2]

2 When will ablation take place? [2]

3 Lakes often form in glacial troughs. The photograph shows an example of this.

What is the name given to this type of lake? [1]

4 Where are tarns found? [2]

5 Label the following diagram. [3]

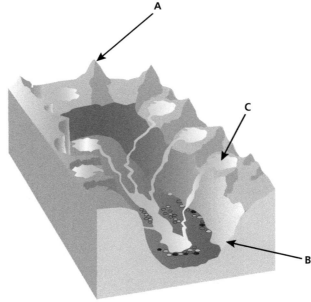

6 What is moraine? [2]

7 Explain how an erratic can be identified. [2]

8 What is a honeypot site? [3]

9 **a)** Name three groups of people who interact in glacial landscapes. [3]

b) How can dog walkers cause a problem in glacial landscapes? [4]

c) Why are visitor centres important in the protection of glacial landscapes? [4]

Rivers and Coasts

1. Name the three processes that take place to shape the landscape around rivers and coasts. [3]

2. Describe the erosional process of corrasion (abrasion). [2]

3. Name one common landform found in the upper course of the river. [1]

4. Name the feature at X below and identify the processes occurring at A and B. [3]

meander

deposition

erosion

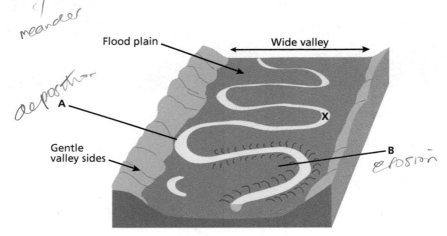

Flood plain

Wide valley

A

X

B

Gentle valley sides

5. Explain what causes a river to flood. [2]

6. Describe the formation of waves. [5]

7. Name features A and B on the diagram below. [2]

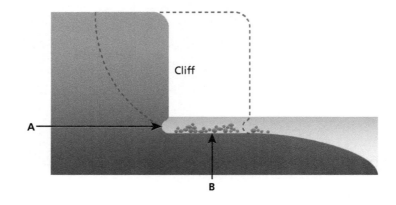

Cliff

A

B

8. Give one advantage and one disadvantage of hard engineering. [2]

Landscapes

1. The photograph shows a built-up city landscape. Why is the built landscape of the world increasing? [2]

2. What was the world population in 2014? [1]

3. Give three ways in which humans exploit natural landscapes. [3]

4. Name one tropical rainforest and outline why it is such an important ecosystem. [3]

5. a) Describe how indigenous people live sustainably in rainforests. [4]

   b) Give three reasons to suggest why indigenous populations are decreasing. [3]

   c) Explain why working with indigenous people can lead to sustainable management of rainforests. [5]

6. Explain how the land in savannah grasslands can be managed to reduce the risk of desertification. [6]

Population

1. The graph shows the actual and predicted world population.

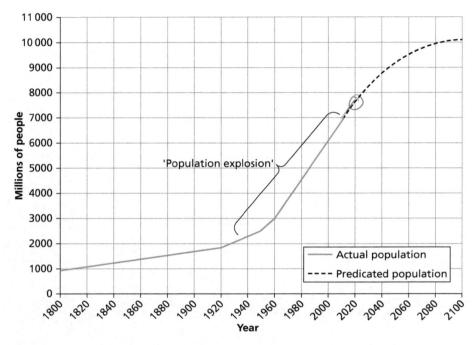

a) What is the present world population? [1]

b) Why is the present growth rate sometimes called a 'population explosion'? [2]

c) What is the world population likely to be in around 100 years? [1]

2. Explain the difference between a 'sparse' population and a 'dense' population. [2]

3. Why do more people than expected live in areas such as Alaska in the USA? [2]

4. Name one country with a high population density and one country with a low population density. [2]

5. What is the difference between a refugee and an illegal immigrant? [2]

6. What causes 'natural' population increase in a country? [1]

7. What is a 'family planning campaign'? [2]

8. Name one population problem linked to age. [2]

Urbanisation

1. **a)** Define the process of urbanisation. [2]

   b) What are the two main causes of urbanisation? [4]

   c) Explain why the mechanisation of farming contributes to urbanisation. [3]

2. What is the difference between suburbanisation and counterurbanisation? [3]

3. **a)** Explain why inner cities have experienced decline. [4]

   b) Give two aims of urban regeneration projects using one example. [4]

4. What is the key difference between HICs' and LICs' experience of urbanisation? [2]

5. **a)** Which of the following are typical characteristics of shanty towns? Tick (✓) the correct options.

   No electricity ☐

   Spacious living conditions ☐

   Running water ☐

   Lack of roads ☐

   Corrugated iron roofs ☐

   Sewage system ☐

   No waste disposal ☐ [4]

   b) Explain the aims of self-help schemes as an approach to improving shanty towns. [4]

6. Study the images below and list the features that characterise a sustainably planned city. [6]

Development 1

You must be able to:

- Define the term development
- Identify indicators that help measure the development process
- Consider factors that slow down the development process
- Identify where developed and developing countries are.

What is Development?

- Development measures how different countries compare to each other in terms of economic, social, technological and cultural levels.
- High levels of development lead to an improved standard of living and quality of life.
- High Income Countries (HICs) are often referred to as *developed* and Low Income Countries (LICs) as *developing*.

Measuring the Development Process

- Different indicators can be used to measure and compare the levels of development in different countries, including social, economic and industrial factors:

Key Point

NIC means Newly Industrialising Country. These are countries such as India and China that have rapidly developing economies.

Examples of Social Indicators	Examples of Economic Indicators	Examples of Industrial Indicators
- Life expectancy: the average age a person will reach. - Infant mortality rates: the number of babies who die before their first birthday. - Literacy rates: the percentage of the population who can read.	- Gross Domestic Product (GDP): the total value of a country's goods and services in one year. - GDP per capita (per person): the GDP divided by the total population of a country.	- Primary industries: Farming, fishing, mining (LIC, for example Ethiopia) - Secondary industries: Manufacturing (NIC, for example China) - Tertiary industries: Services, banking, IT (HIC, for example the UK) - As a country becomes more economically developed it will move towards more tertiary industries.

Why are some Countries Slower to Develop?

- There are human and physical factors that have a negative impact on the development process in many countries.

- Human factors include:
  - Past colonial activities stripped many LICs of their resources (to the benefit of the colonial powers).
  - Poor governance may mean that money is held with a few powerful people and not used to develop the health, education and employment of the population.
  - Disease affects people's ability to work or go to school.
  - LICs' exports are mainly primary produce, which is of a lower value than the goods they import from HICs, leading to a **trade deficit**.
  - HICs control the price they pay LICs for their primary produce.
  - Many LICs borrowed money from HICs so much of their GDP is spent paying off the **debt**.
- Physical factors include:
  - Many countries (e.g. those in sub-Saharan Africa) suffer from conditions like drought, which leaves soils infertile and unproductive.
  - Natural disasters such as floods or earthquakes mean money must be spent on recovery.
  - Many African countries are landlocked (surrounded by other countries) so access to ports and trade routes is difficult.
  - Access to valuable natural resources may be difficult or expensive.

> **Key Point**
>
> These factors must be considered and understood if countries are to be helped to develop effectively.

Where are the Developed and Developing Countries?

- The North/South divide refers to the fact that most of the countries in the northern hemisphere are developed, whereas many countries in the southern hemisphere are less developed.
- The **Brandt Line** is an imaginary line that divides the developed north from the less developed south.
- The Brandt Line is misleading and outdated because many countries below the line are NICs (India and China).

Brandt line

HIC
LIC

> **Quick Test**
>
> 1. What type of indicators help us to understand how developed a country is?
> 2. Give one example of a social indicator.
> 3. Why is there a trade deficit in many developing countries?
> 4. Explain the concept of the Brandt Line.

> **Key Words**
>
> indicators
> trade deficit
> debt
> Brandt Line

Development 2

You must be able to:

- Understand the importance of composite indicators
- Recall the aims of the Millennium Development Goals
- Consider the problems of aid
- Define and understand the importance of sustainable development.

Composite Indicators

- Development is measured by combining a variety of indicators that examine the economic, social and cultural characteristics of a country. These are known as 'composite indicators'.
- The **Human Development Index** (HDI) measures life expectancy, knowledge (adult literacy and education) and standard of living (GDP per capita).
- The HDI is a more meaningful measure of a country's level of development than looking at indicators separately because it shows the connection between economic and social development.
- Nigeria, for example, has a GDP that is almost twice as large as that of New Zealand but has a very low HDI figure of just 0.471 compared to New Zealand's 0.919 (the fourth highest in the world). This leads us to consider the human and physical factors that are affecting Nigeria's ability to develop.

> **Key Point**
>
> The closer the Human Development Index figure is to 1, the more developed the country; Norway, for example, scores 0.955.

Nigeria   442976
Norway   366386
Ireland   399064
SAfrica   282558

The United Nations Millennium Development Goals

- The United Nations (UN) is an organisation formed in 1945 that works for international peace and security. Most of the world's countries are members.
- In 2000 the UN agreed to eight goals aimed at promoting development globally.
- These goals focus on meeting basic human rights that are needed for a higher quality of life. They include:
  - universal education
  - child health
  - reduced child mortality
  - an end to poverty and hunger.
- Countries are scored annually on their progress in reaching these targets by 2015.

> **Key Point**
>
> Basic human rights are the rights of each person on the planet to health, education, shelter and security.

Australia 1334688   0.938   6th
India   2592   0.647   129th

Problems of Aid

- Many HICs give money to LICs to assist their development process; this is known as aid.
- But aid is often given with conditions attached. These conditions often benefit the donor more than the recipient:
  - Aid may be given in the form of large projects that are run by the HIC, meaning profits may be greater for the donor.
  - Large projects may be undertaken without proper consideration of their effects on the environment.
  - Corrupt LIC governments may prevent the aid from going where it is needed most.
  - Aid may lead to dependency on the HIC.
  - Aid may be in the form of loans that result in LICs struggling even more than before as their debt repayments increase.

Sustainable Development

- If development is to be successful and sustainable then money must form just one part of the development process.
- Economic sustainability, social sustainability and environmental sustainability must all be considered.
- Sustainable development is development that meets the needs of the present without compromising the ability of future generations to meet their own needs.

Fair Trade

- Fair trade ensures that trade is beneficial to the LIC and not controlled unfairly by the HICs they trade with.
- The Fair Trade Foundation was developed in the UK to ensure this happens.
- When a product in the shops has the FAIRTRADE symbol it means:
  - the farmer was paid a fair price
  - a percentage of the money paid goes towards improving the local community and environment
  - the product has a stable position within the global market.

Key Point

Fair trade contributes to sustainable development by assisting social, environmental and economic progress.

Quick Test

1. What are composite indicators?
2. Why can GDP be a misleading measure of development?
3. Give two problems of aid.
4. Define sustainable development.

Key Words

Human Development Index
donor
recipient
dependency
sustainable development
fair trade

Economic Activity 1

You must be able to:

- Classify economic activities into different groups
- Know what sort of jobs people do in different countries
- Know where people get their food from.

Economic Activity

- Economic activity is defined as human actions that deal with the production, distribution and consumption of goods and services.
- Individuals and companies carry out economic activities to earn money.
  - Individuals use the money to live – to pay for goods and services.
  - In the case of a company, the aim is to make a profit.
- There are three main kinds of economic activity:

Primary Activities	Secondary Activities	Tertiary Activities
Primary activities involve natural resources, such as minerals, timber, fossil fuels and food. The products can be grown or dug out of the ground and then sold. Some are processed into other things (oil is used to produce fertiliser and other chemicals) but many can be used as they are (bananas).	**Secondary activities** involve making or **manufacturing** things from natural resources. This usually happens in factories. Examples include making bread from wheat and other ingredients, making paper from trees, building a car using many different materials (metal, plastics, rubber, and glass).	**Tertiary Activities** involve providing a **service** for other people or organisations. Examples include teaching, nursing, police services, estate agents, and all types of shop work.

- In the UK and other HICs:
  - Most people (70–80%) work in the tertiary sector.
  - Many secondary activities employ few people, as machines and robots do much of the work.
  - Only a tiny percentage of people work in primary activities such as farming and mining.

- In the LICs, there is a great deal of variation:
  - In some LICs, such as Nigeria, the majority of people still work on the land growing their own food.
  - In others, such as China, a growing number now live in cities and work in factories.

Farming and Food Production

- In LICs people still work on the land to provide their own food. If they have a small surplus, they may sell it at a local market. The money can be used to buy other goods and services. Such farms are usually small and inefficient.
- Many LICs have now developed large modern farms that provide food not for local people but for HICs, such as the UK and USA.
- In the UK we buy food from around the world so that all types of food are available all year round.
- Although we can grow all of these in the UK, examples of imported food include strawberries, asparagus, sweetcorn, green beans and apples.
- Farms in LICs also grow non-food products:
  - cotton
  - oilseed
  - flowers
  - medicinal herbs.
- Many of these non-food items are exported to industrial countries where they are processed into useful products such as cotton for clothing, or oilseed for biofuels.
- In the UK we grow about 60% of the food we need and the rest is imported. We couldn't grow all our own food as things such as oranges, sweet potatoes and rice need a much hotter climate to grow.
- Most UK farms are very modern and highly mechanised. They use large amounts of chemicals to make the crops grow and to kill off bugs and weeds. Some farms are organic, which means they use no chemicals.
- **Arable** farms grow the plants that we eat (potatoes, carrots, wheat, etc.) and the pastoral farms rear the animals that provide us with eggs, milk and meat.

 Key Point

In the UK we grow about two-thirds of the food we eat. The rest is imported from around the world.

 Key Words

primary activity
secondary activity
manufacturing
tertiary activity
service
arable
pastoral

Quick Test

1. Why do people carry out economic activities?
2. What kind of economic activity is nursing?
3. What is a food surplus?
4. Why do farmers grow cotton?

Economic Activity 2

You must be able to:

- Explain the different things that are needed for a factory
- Outline where different products are made
- Explain what kind of work is done in the tertiary sector.

Manufacturing Industry

- Humans have always made the items they need from natural resources. Over the last 200 years most manufacturing has been done in factories and workshops.
- It is cheaper and more efficient to make lots of the same items in a factory so we now have factories that specialise in making particular goods such as computers, cars and smart phones.
- Factories need land to build on, natural resources to make their products, energy to power the factory, labour (workers) and good transport links to move products to market.
- In the past, factories needed lots of labour but today much of the work is mechanised, i.e. done by machines. In car factories, specialised robots do a lot of the repetitive or dangerous jobs.

Manufacturing Industry in NICs

- Although the UK still has a manufacturing industry – we make cars, clothes, chemicals and food products for example – much manufacturing is now done in LICs and NICs (Newly Industrialising Countries).
- In countries such as China, Brazil and Mexico workers are paid much less so factories have lower labour costs. Land may also be cheaper and environmental laws not so strict about pollution and waste products.
- Many textiles (clothing) were made in the UK in the past but today the majority of the world's textiles come from Asia.
- Many UK companies with well-known labels, such as New Look, GAP, Monsoon, River Island, Primark, TK Maxx, Topshop, Burton, and Miss Selfridge import their clothes from Asia.
- In the past, there have been complaints of factory workers being badly treated with very low wages and long hours of work without a break. Such factories are called 'sweatshops'.
- Another important industry are the high-tech factories that make computers, tablets, smart phones and TVs. Japan and the USA were famous in the past for making many of these products but many Japanese and American companies have now moved their factories to Taiwan, Singapore, Malaysia and China.

> **Key Point**
>
> A large amount of manufacturing now takes place in NICs where labour costs are lower.

> **Key Point**
>
> India, Bangladesh and China have large numbers of textile factories employing millions of people, mainly women.

- Some NICs have now become world leaders in high-tech products. The best example of this is Samsung in South Korea. In 2012, Samsung Electronics became the world's largest mobile phone maker.

Providing a Service

- In the HICs the majority of jobs are now in the tertiary sector – providing a service for other people and organisations.
- The sort of work carried out in the service industries varies from low-skilled and low paid jobs (shop assistants, office cleaners, care workers, security guards, etc.) through to highly skilled professionals who require degree qualifications and years of training (lawyers, doctors, dentists, vets, etc.).
- One of the most important service sectors in the UK is the retail or shopping sector, which provides jobs for over three million people.
- There are many different kinds of work in retail from sales assistant, through customer services and marketing, to finance and management.
- People working in retail may be located in town centres but also increasingly in large shopping centres such as Bluewater in Kent, Meadowhall in Sheffield and the Trafford Centre in Manchester.
- Many high streets now have identical sets of shops with well-known names as smaller family businesses have increasingly closed down.
- Supermarkets have taken over from many small butchers, bakers and fruit and vegetable shops.

> **Key Point**
>
> Service jobs are the most common kind of work in the UK but many people earn very low wages.

> **Quick Test**
>
> 1. Why do factories need good transport links?
> 2. What is an NIC?
> 3. Name one high-tech product.
> 4. How important are service jobs in the UK?

> **Key Words**
>
> labour
> mechanised
> Newly Industrialising Countries
> textiles
> high-tech
> retail

Natural Resources 1

You must be able to:

- Explain what natural resources are and give examples
- Understand the difference between renewable and non-renewable resources
- Know about different kinds of trees and what they are used for.

What are Natural Resources?

- **Natural resources** are resources found in nature. Humans need these natural resources in order to survive and to enjoy a good quality of life.
- Some natural resources are **renewable** and, used carefully, will go on being available for many years into the future. For example, plants and animals will reproduce themselves so long as we do not deplete their numbers too drastically.
- Unfortunately, humans often don't use resources carefully, which means that there is a danger they could disappear.
- For example, in the North Sea, overfishing has reduced fish numbers to such an extent that there are not enough left to replenish the stocks. Fishing boats now have to sail further away from the UK to find fish.
- A **sustainable** use of resources means using them carefully so there are enough for future generations to use.
- An example of sustainable use would be to plant two young trees every time we cut down a mature tree to use the timber. This will ensure a plentiful supply of trees for future generations.
- Some natural resources are **non-renewable**. They have taken millions of years to be created and once used up, there will be no more.
- The fossil fuels (coal, oil and natural gas) are important examples of non-renewable resources.
- To make non-renewable resources last longer, we have to either use smaller quantities or where possible, try to **recycle** them. Many metals can be recycled and used again.

> **Key Point**
>
> Humans need to use natural resources carefully (sustainably) so that they are still around for future generations.

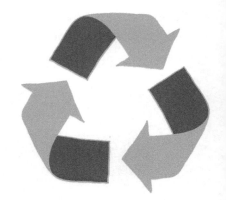

Forestry Resources

- Wood has always been an important natural resource. People use it for building their homes, for fuel and for paper making.
- Coniferous trees are softwood trees:
  - They grow in areas with cool climates such as Northern Europe, Canada and northern Russia.
  - They are quick growing (25–30 years to reach full size) and ideal for building and for paper making.

- Millions of softwood trees are planted and cut down each year. Coniferous trees are not in short supply as they grow very quickly.
- Deciduous trees, such as oaks, are hardwood trees:
  - They grow in both temperate and tropical areas such as the UK and Brazil.
  - They are slow growing (80–120 years to reach full size) and the timber is prized for high value products such as furniture and ornaments.
- The tropical rainforests contain hardwood trees such as mahogany and teak.
- To find the rare and valuable trees, whole areas of rainforest are cleared. This destroys the natural environment where other plants, animals and insects live.
- Some people believe that the rainforests should be preserved but the local people need work and the timber that is exported earns money for the government to pay for schools, roads and hospitals.
- A single teak tree may be worth over £10 000.

> ### Key Point
>
> Softwood trees can be grown quickly to replace trees that are cut down but hardwood trees can take 100 years to reach full size so it is difficult to replace hardwood forests.

(handwritten notes:)
Conifers   Deciduous
softwood   hardwood
fast-growing   slow growing
used for   used for
making paper   making furniture

Coniferous tree

Deciduous tree

Tropical rainforest

> #### Quick Test
>
> 1. How are natural resources created?
> 2. Why do we need natural resources?
> 3. Name one natural resource.
> 4. Will natural resources always be available for humans to use?

> ### Key Words
>
> natural resources
> renewable
> sustainable
> non-renewable
> recycle

Natural Resources 2

You must be able to:

- Understand why there are now declining numbers of fish left in the seas and oceans
- Know what the different kinds of fossil fuels are and where they come from
- Know what different fossil fuels are used for.

Resources from the Sea

- The seas, oceans and lakes around the world have always been used by humans to find food and other resources.
- The main source of food from the sea is fish. Humans also collect shellfish, prawns, seaweed, coral and salt from the sea.
- A large percentage of the fish living in the seas and oceans have now disappeared due to overfishing. It is getting harder to find fish in large numbers in areas near to where people live.
- A lot of the fish that we now eat comes from fish farms. The fish are reared in indoor tanks and then put into shallow lakes or offshore in cages where they are fed artificially with pellets of fish food. Salmon and trout are good examples of fish reared in this way.
- Although a few small, local fishing boats still exist, most sea fishing is done by huge factory ships and trawlers. These catch fish indiscriminately in huge nets, whether useful or not. Useful fish are processed and frozen at sea in the factory ships – anything unwanted is thrown back into the sea dead or dying.

> ### Key Point
>
> Many natural supplies of fish have now disappeared due to overfishing and we depend increasingly on fish farms for our food.

Fish farm

Energy Resources

- Fossil fuels have provided humans with fuel for the last 150 years.
- Coal has been mined for much longer than this but became important during the Industrial Revolution when it was used in a variety of ways:
  - in furnaces to smelt iron and later steel
  - in coal fires to heat homes
  - in steam engines that powered factory machines and railway engines.
- Today coal is still an important fuel in the power stations that generate our electricity. About 33% of our electricity is generated by burning coal. This creates a problem since coal produces pollution, including greenhouse gases that contribute to global warming.

Power station

- About three-quarters of the coal used in the UK is now imported into the UK from other countries since most of our coal mines have been closed down (over half of imported coal comes from Russia).
- The most important fossil fuel is now natural gas. 40% of our electricity comes from burning natural gas in power stations. Natural gas is also used in homes for heating and cooking.
- Like coal, we import an increasing amount of our natural gas (around 50%). It arrives by pipeline from other European countries or by tanker from the Middle East.
- Oil or petroleum is only rarely used in power stations but it is one of our most important natural resources. Oil is piped to refineries where it is converted into many different products such as petrol, diesel, engine oil, plastics, fertilisers, pesticides and a variety of important drugs such as aspirin.
- Both oil and natural gas are found under the North Sea so they are collected by drilling rigs that are connected by pipeline to the coast. Both of these natural resources are slowly running out.

> **Key Point**
>
> Fossil fuels are a non-renewable resource but we depend on them to produce electricity and many of our everyday essential items.

North Sea Oil Rig

> **Quick Test**
>
> 1. What is the main natural resource that we get from the sea?
> 2. What fossil fuel was used to power machines 100 years ago?
> 3. What is made in a power station?
> 4. What is an import?

> **Key Words**
>
> overfishing
> fish farm
> factory ship
> fossil fuel
> power station

Ordnance Survey Maps 1

You must be able to:

- Identify direction
- Calculate distance using scales
- Locate places using grid references (four-figure and six-figure)
- Understand the relief (shape) of the land using contour lines.

Direction

- Direction is given on a map using the points of the compass.
- The cardinal points of a compass going clockwise are north, east, south and west. You can remember their order using the mnemonic 'Naughty Elephants Squirt Water'.
- North is always at the top of an Ordnance Survey (OS) map.
- On OS maps light blue grid lines run from north to south and from east to west.

Scale

- Scale is indicated on an OS map using a ratio, a scale line and the size of the grid squares.
- The most common scales on OS maps are 1:50 000 and 1:25 000.
  - 1:50 000 means that the map is 50 000 times smaller than the places that it shows, so that 2 cm on the map is equal to 1 km in reality. The grid squares on the map are 2 cm x 2 cm.
  - 1:25 000 means that the map is 25 000 times smaller than the places that it shows, so that 4 cm on the map is equal to 1 km in reality. The grid squares on the map are 4 cm x 4 cm.

> **Key Point**
>
> Grid squares are always 1 km² on an OS map.

Measuring Distance

- There are a number of ways to measure distance on a map: one of the easiest is to count the number of grid squares from one point to another. This is a quick way of finding the distance between places to the nearest kilometre.
- Another method is to use a piece of paper and lay it against the scale line printed on the map.

 Place the paper between the two places you want to measure.

2 Mark the two places on the paper.

3 Place the paper along the scale line at the bottom of the map, with the mark indicating the first place at the zero on the scale line.

4 Write down the distance on the scale line indicated by your mark for the second place.

Four-Figure Grid References

- Four-figure grid references are used to locate an area of 1 km² on an OS map. This is the area of one grid square.
- To find the four-figure grid reference of a square on an OS map:
  - **1** Go along the bottom of the map until you reach the line at the left-hand side of the square.
  - **2** Write down the two numbers of this line.
  - **3** Go up the side of the map until you reach the line at the bottom of the square.
  - **4** Write down the two numbers of this line.
  - **5** You should now have a four-figure grid reference.

Key Point

Remember to use the numbers at the bottom of the map first followed by the numbers at the side of the map. Say to yourself 'along the corridor and up the stairs'.

Uffington Village: Grid Reference 3089

Go up second

Go along first

Key Words

compass
cardinal points
Ordnance Survey (OS)
grid lines
scale line
grid references

Quick Test

1. Which direction is always at the top of an OS map?
2. How large are the grid squares on a 1:50 000 OS map?
3. What size area does a four-figure grid reference locate?

Ordnance Survey Maps 2

You must be able to:

- Locate places using six-figure grid references
- Understand the relief (shape) of the land using contour lines
- Use a key to understand map symbols effectively.

Six-Figure Grid References

- Six-figure grid references are used to locate an area of 100 m x 100 m on an OS map.
- To find a six-figure grid reference of an area on an OS map:

    1 Go along the bottom of the map until you reach the line at the left-hand side of the grid square that the area is in.

    2 Write down the two numbers of this line.

    3 Divide the bottom of the grid square into 10, with 5 being in the middle of the square.

    4 Count along the bottom of the grid square until you reach the area, then write down the number you have got to.

    5 Go up the side of the map until you reach the line at the bottom of the grid square that the area is in.

    6 Write down the two numbers of this line.

    7 Divide the side of the grid square into 10, with 5 being in the middle of the square.

    8 Count up the side of the grid square until you reach the area, then write down the number you have got to.

    9 You should now have a six-figure grid reference.

Relief

- **Relief** is the height and shape of land.
- Relief is shown on an OS map using **contour lines** and **spot heights**.
- Contour lines are thin brown lines that join up places of equal height above sea level; they are usually drawn in 10-metre intervals.
- Spot heights are points on a map with a precise measurement of the height above sea level in metres printed on the map.
- **Triangulation points** are used by surveyors to measure the height of the land; they are indicated on an OS map with a blue triangle and a height above sea level in metres printed next to it.

Key Point

Remember that the half-way point from one side of a grid square to the other is 5 therefore the grid reference for the middle of a grid square will always be xx5xx5.

Key Point

The closer contour lines are together, the steeper the slope will be.

contour line

spot height

Map Symbols

- Map symbols can be divided into different types to make them easier to understand. If you are unsure what a map symbol means always look it up in the key (a key is shown below).
- Footpaths are marking using solid or dashed red lines on a 1:50 000 map and green lines on a 1:25 000 map.
- Forests and woods are shown by blocks of green containing symbols representing the different types of tree: deciduous, coniferous or mixed.
- Buildings are drawn as pink rectangles and important buildings are edged in a thick black line.
- Some buildings are drawn as symbols such as churches, lighthouses and windmills.
- OS maps also use abbreviations for some important buildings including:
  - PH = public house
  - Sch = school
- Tourist information is shown on OS maps using blue symbols.

Key Point

1:25 000 maps are large-scale maps, which means that they show more detail than 1:50 000 maps. For example 1:25 000 maps show field boundaries (hedges and fences) as thin black lines, which makes it much easier to navigate on a walk, whereas 1:50 000 maps do not.

Key Point

There is a wider range of tourist information on 1:25 000 scale maps in comparison to 1:50 000 maps.

Quick Test

1. By how much do you have to divide the side of a grid square when you are working out a six-figure grid reference?
2. What is the usual interval between contour lines?
3. What colour are motorways on an OS map?
4. What does PH stand for on an OS map?

Key Words

relief
contour lines
spot heights
triangulation points

Review Questions

Rivers and Coasts

1. What are the three main stages along a river's course? [3]

2. a) What are the four main processes of erosion? [4]

   b) Name one landform resulting from erosion. [1]

   c) Name one landform resulting from deposition. [1]

3. Say whether each cause of flooding is a human cause or a physical cause by drawing lines to match the boxes.

   | Saturated soil |

   | Urbanisation |

   | Impermeable rock |
          | Human cause |

   | Heavy rain |
          | Physical cause |

   | Deforestation | [5]

4. What features of rock will affect rates of weathering and erosion along coastlines? [2]

5. What is the difference between constructive waves and destructive waves? [2]

6. Draw lines to match the type of rock to its example.

   | Chalk |

   | Soft rock |
   | Sandstone |

   | Hard rock |
   | Granite | [3]

7. What process transports material along the coastline? [1]

8. Suggest two groups of people who might disagree about how the coast should be managed. Suggest how the groups might disagree. [3]

Landscapes

1 **a)** Define the term 'exploit'. [2]

   b) Give two examples of humans exploiting natural landscapes. [2]

2 Why is overpopulation a problem for natural landscapes? [3]

3 **a)** What is the name of the gas that is released when rainforests are burned?
      Tick (✓) the correct option.

   Oxygen ☐

   Methane ☐

   Nitrogen ☐

   Carbon dioxide ☐ [1]

   b) Why does this contribute to global warming? [1]

4 **a)** Which two characteristics of climate change can lead to desertification?
      Tick (✓) the correct options.

   Increased wet periods ☐

   Increased dry periods ☐

   Lower temperatures ☐

   Less rainfall ☐ [2]

   b) Give two characteristics of soil that has suffered desertification. [2]

5 **a)** Explain how deforestation leads to soil erosion. [2]

   b) Why does planting trees prevent soil erosion? [2]

6 **a)** Why are rainforests being removed? [2]

   b) Define the term indigenous. [2]

   c) Why are indigenous people so important for the future of rainforests? [3]

Review Questions

Population

1 The graph shows how the world population is growing.

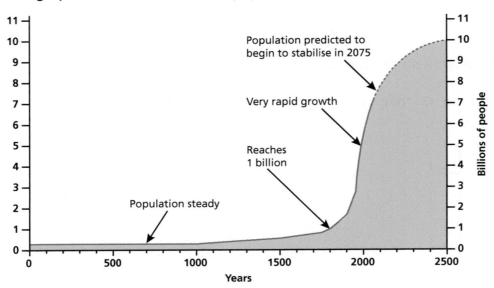

Population predicted to begin to stabilise in 2075

Very rapid growth

Reaches 1 billion

Population steady

Billions of people

Years

a) Why is the world population growing very quickly at the moment? [2]

b) Why is it likely, eventually, to level out at around 10 billion people? [3]

2 Name two areas of the world which have a sparse population and explain why so few people live there. [4]

3 Which area has the highest population density? Give data to support your answer.

A London

B Highlands of Scotland [2]

4 Why might a civil war lead to many refugees arriving in a neighbouring country? [2]

5 What is happening to birth rates in most LICs? Tick (✓) the correct option.

Rising ☐

Falling ☐

Staying the same ☐ [1]

6 Why do many HICs have high death rates? [2]

7 Why are many migrants from Eastern Europe coming to live in the UK? [2]

Urbanisation

1. **a)** What do HIC and LIC stand for? [2]

   b) Which group of countries are experiencing rapid urbanisation at the moment? [1]

2. **a)** Why did people start to move away from cities in the UK? [3]

   b) Name two processes that illustrate this movement away from city centres. [2]

3. **a)** Which of the following are characteristics of urban decline? Tick (✓) the correct options.

   Full employment ☐

   Crime ☐

   High quality housing ☐

   Abandoned shops ☐

   Derelict factories ☐ [3]

   b) What is urban regeneration? Give an example. [3]

4. The photo shows a megacity.

   a) Define a megacity. [1]

   b) Where are megacities growing most rapidly? [1]

5. What three aspects must be considered when managing cities? [3]

6. How can homes be energy efficient? [4]

Practice Questions

Development

1. a) What does development measure? [1]

   b) What types of indicator can be used to measure development? [2]

   c) Give three examples of social indicators. [3]

   d) Give two examples of economic indicators. [2]

2. Which types of industry dominate in LICs? Give examples. [4]

3. Explain how physical factors can influence the level of development in LICs. [4]

4. The image shows the Brandt line. Explain why the Brandt Line is no longer a meaningful description of developed and developing countries. [2]

5. Why is the Human Development Index a useful way of understanding development? [4]

6. Use the following key words to complete the paragraph about the problems of giving aid.

   environment   recipient   attached   corrupt   dependency   donor

   Aid is often given with conditions ...., which often benefit the ....

   more than the ....

   Large aid projects don't always consider the fragile .... in which they're built.

   .... LIC governments may prevent the aid from going where it is needed most. Aid may

   lead to aid .... on the HIC. [6]

7. a) Explain the concept of sustainable development. [5]

   b) How does fair trade contribute to sustainable development? [5]

Economic Activity

1   Why do companies carry out economic activities?   [1]

2   Draw lines between the boxes to match each of these workers to the sector they are classified as.

| Teacher | | Primary |
| Coal miner | | Secondary |
| Baker | | Tertiary | [3]

3   a) Give two examples of natural resources produced by primary workers.   [2]

b) Name two examples of people working in the tertiary sector.   [2]

c) Calculate the missing percentages at A, B and C below.

	Primary	Secondary	Tertiary
Nigeria	A	10%	20%
China	38%	B	34%
United Kingdom	2%	18%	C

[3]

4   a) Name two farm products that can be grown in the UK but are often imported.   [2]

b) How much of the food eaten in the UK is grown by UK farmers?   [1]

5   Fill in the missing words to complete the following sentence.

Factories need land to build on, _____ _____ to make their products, _____ to power the factory.   [3]

6   a) Name two countries where most clothing is now manufactured.   [2]

b) What is a 'sweatshop' factory?   [2]

7   Which of these jobs would be low-skilled and low paid? Tick (✓) the correct options.

Office cleaner ☐

Dentist ☐

Security guard ☐

Teacher ☐   [2]

Practice Questions

Natural Resources

1. Where are natural resources found? [1]

2. If we make use of our natural resources in a sustainable way, why is that a good thing? [2]

3. What is the problem with non-renewable natural resources? [1]

4. Give two reasons why wood is an important natural resource. [2]

5. a) How long does it take for a coniferous tree to reach full size? Tick (✓) the correct option.

   25–30 years ☐

   55–60 years ☐

   75–80 years ☐ [1]

   b) Why is there no shortage of coniferous trees? [2]

6. a) Name one type of hardwood tree that grows in the rainforest. [1]

   b) Why is it important that some of the rainforest is preserved? [2]

7. a) What is a fish farm? [2]

   b) What happens in a factory ship? [2]

8. a) Where does most of the coal now used in our power stations come from? Tick (✓) the correct option.

   Morocco ☐

   Spain ☐

   Russia ☐

   Japan ☐

   Greenland ☐ [1]

   b) Where, apart from power stations, is natural gas used? [2]

Ordnance Survey Maps

1 Study this extract of the Landranger 1:50 000 Ordnance Survey Map based around Newquay.

a) What is the four-figure reference of the square that contains Penhale Point? [2]

b) Give the four-figure references for:

   i) the village of Cubert   **ii)** the leisure park in Newquay   **iii)** the wind farm [6]

c) Name the villages in the following grid squares:

   i) 8256   **ii)** 7653   **iii)** 7853 [6]

d) You have just stayed at a hotel at 8062. Your friend is in a hotel at 7760.
   What is the straight line distance between the two hotels? [2]

Geographic Information Systems 1

You must be able to:

- Understand what a Geographic Information System (GIS) does
- Understand how a GIS can be used in real life
- Know the different sorts of data used in a GIS.

GIS Overview

- A Geographic Information System (GIS) brings together hardware, software, and data. A GIS can be used to capture, manage, analyse, and display all forms of information that is georeferenced.
- At a simple level, a GIS can be used to view data on maps. The data can be changed, analysed and viewed in different ways to help gain an understanding of geographical patterns and relationships.
- In order to use a GIS, you need:
  - A computer or tablet.
  - GIS software to organise the data.
  - Digital data, including map data and other sorts of data such as census information.
- Geographic Information Systems have been used in the real world for many years now. Examples include:
  - The police service use GIS to plot crime patterns, enabling them to focus on crime prevention in key areas.
  - The ambulance service use GIS to keep track of where each ambulance is positioned and which one can respond most quickly to an emergency call.
  - Water, gas and electricity companies use GIS to map the positions of underground pipes and cables so that they know where it is safe to dig. They also record the condition of the pipes and cables.
  - Supermarkets use GIS to plan their deliveries. All supermarket goods come from giant warehouses and hundreds of lorries transport the goods across the UK each day to the different supermarkets.

> **Key Point**
>
> A Geographic Information System (GIS) is a combination of computer hardware, GIS software, and digital data.

How does a GIS work?

- A GIS consists of layers of information (like sheets of paper) stacked on top of each other. The GIS software has a key that allows you to switch layers on or off. Layers can also be made transparent so that you can see the layer beneath.

GIS layers

People

Roads

Relief

Land use

The real world

- The base layer is usually a digital map but it could be a photo or satellite image.
- The features on the digital map are divided into four types:
  1. **Points** are symbols that represent a feature at a particular point location, e.g. a trig point that shows the top of a mountain.
  2. **Lines** are symbols that show things like roads and rivers.
  3. **Polygons** cover an area and may be a regular shape such as a square to represent a building or an irregular shape to represent something like a lake.
  4. **Text** is used for the names of places, or landscape features, e.g. Mount Snowdon, River Thames, Heathrow Airport.
- Digital maps will show both natural and manmade features. The relief or shape of the land is shown by numbered contour lines. This data can be used to show the land as a 3D image with hills and valleys.
- In the UK digital map data is created and published by the Ordnance Survey (OS). They produce paper maps as well as digital data for computers, tablets, smartphones and satellite navigation systems (sat navs).

Quick Test

1. What do the letters GIS stand for?
2. What do the police use a GIS for?
3. What might a line on a digital map show?
4. Who produces digital maps in the UK?

Key Words

Geographic Information System
layer of information
point
line
polygon

Geographic Information Systems 2

You must be able to:

- Outline what kinds of online GIS are available for free
- Understand how you can use these geotechnologies in different ways
- Know how to use and add data to Google Earth.

Geotechnologies

- It is now possible to use many different kinds of **geotechnologies** (geographical technologies) for free online.
  - Some local councils, for example, put all their digital data into online GIS systems, providing local maps showing leisure facilities, waste disposal facilities, parks and open spaces, local footpaths and shopping centres.
- Online GIS provided by commercial organisations and local authorities allow you to view different kinds of data but you cannot enter your own data or alter the data shown on the maps.
  - An exception to this is Wikimapia, a publicly created map that allows users to add features to help build up the information presented.

> **Key Point**
>
> Many GIS systems are now available for free online so that the public can access map data.

Google Earth

- A good way of doing some GIS work for free is to use Google Earth (GE). Google Earth is a **virtual globe** with maps and a variety of GIS data that can be added as layers and which also allows you to add your own data.
- In Google Earth you can zoom through different scales from the initial global view, through national to local scales. In this way, you can see where places are located and how they relate to other places. This helps to develop your spatial understanding in geography.

- Google Earth has built in layers for borders, roads, weather, land use and much more. You can choose which layers you want to view in the Layers Panel.
- One of the most exciting geographical features is that you can view 'live' layers in which the data is regularly updated. In this way you can see changing cloud cover or where the latest earthquake has happened.
- Most of the data shown in Google Earth comes from high resolution satellite imagery and as you zoom in, you can see settlements, roads and land use. At a local level, satellite images are replaced by aerial photos taken from aircraft. These allow you to see much finer detail such as your house and garden!
- Google Earth has a timeline feature that allows you to view a sequence of superimposed images showing how an area has changed over time. In this way, you can see how a city such as New Delhi in India has grown in size or large areas of the tropical rainforest in Brazil have been lost.
- Google Earth allows you to plot your own data and save the maps. You can add:
  - placemarks
  - polygons
  - paths
  - images
  - text boxes
  - videos.
- You can also do 'tours' in Google Earth that allow you to fly automatically from one part of the world to another. You can even fly under the sea and view the ocean floor!

Fieldwork 1

You must be able to:

- Explain what is meant by fieldwork (or LOtC)
- Understand how to make fieldwork successful
- Know how to collect different kinds of data.

Fieldwork Overview

- **Fieldwork**, sometimes called **Learning Outside the Classroom** (LOtC) is a vital part of work in geography. It involves working outside the classroom in order to observe phenomena or to collect data about the real world.
- Fieldwork or LOtC can happen in the school grounds, in the local neighbourhood, a different part of the UK or most adventurous of all – overseas fieldwork in another country.
- The fieldwork process usually involves work outside and then work back in the classroom:
  - collating data
  - displaying data
  - analysing data
  - drawing conclusions.
- Most fieldwork is linked to **enquiry-based learning** which means using a question as a starting point and then trying to find evidence to answer that question.
- For successful fieldwork it is important to have:
  - Good planning.
  - Proper equipment, footwear and clothing.
  - A positive attitude to the work.
  - Health and safety at all times.
  - Co-operation – much fieldwork involves group work.

Data Collection

- Data is the information we collect when working outside the classroom. Accuracy of data collection is very important. You need to learn how to use tools and fieldwork equipment.
- There are many different ways to collect data. These include using our eyes and recording what we see on paper. This could be a description of an actual object (a tall, white chalk cliff) or our **perception** (I think this area looks dangerous/untidy/unfriendly). Perception is about how we feel.
- We can take photos or sound recordings to record what we see and hear. It is helpful if these are **georeferenced**. This means recording the location using co-ordinates (latitude/longitude or a grid reference). Some equipment does this automatically.

Key Point

Fieldwork, or Learning Outside the Classroom, is a very important part of work in Geography. It allows you to experience the real world.

Key Point

A lot of data is collectively systematically, i.e. at regular intervals (every 5 minutes or every 10 metres).

- In different types of fieldwork, we might measure different things:
  - Urban study (e.g. types of housing, amount of litter, noise levels).
  - Shopping study (e.g. types of shops, number of pedestrians, size of shop frontage).
  - River study (e.g. width of stream, stream velocity, slope angle).
  - Beach study (e.g. width of beach, pebble size, types of waves).
  - Microclimate study (e.g. temperature, wind speed, sunshine/shade).
  - Soil study (e.g. soil depth, soil texture, soil moisture).
- Data collection can involve using special equipment such as a wind vane (to measure wind direction), a flow meter (to measure velocity or speed of river flow) and a quadrat (a one-metre square metal grid).
- Data collection can involve us making judgements. To help quantify the judgement, we may use something like a bi-polar scale:

Key Point

There are many different ways to collect data. It is important to be accurate and learn how to use tools and equipment.

| Clean | +5 | +4 | +3 | +2 | +1 | 0 | −1 | −2 | −3 | −4 | −5 | Dirty |

- Questionnaires are a very useful way to collect information from people. They can be anonymous (no names) but should include some personal details such as age group (0–16, 17–35, 36–50, over 50) and gender (male/female). This allows us to see if different groups of people give different answers.
- Questionnaires can have open questions which give space for people to give an opinion or they can have closed questions which give people several things to choose from and then tick one box.

Do you think the supermarket should be built on this site?

_____

_____

Open question

Which is your favourite take-away food?

a) Burger King [ ]   **b)** McDonalds [ ]

Closed question

Quick Test

1. What do the letters LOtC mean?
2. Why is co-operation important for successful fieldwork?
3. What is a grid reference an example of?
4. What is a wind vane used for?

Key Words

fieldwork
Learning Outside the Classroom
enquiry-based learning
perception
georeference
bi-polar scale

Fieldwork 2

You must be able to:

- Know why data should be presented on maps and as graphs
- Understand which method of data presentation is most appropriate.

Data Presentation

- Data collected during fieldwork can be presented in many different ways. It is helpful to organise the data so that it can be analysed and conclusions can be drawn.
- Presenting data on maps is an important geographical skill. Sometimes we want to show change over time. This can be done by using a **historical map** from the OS (Ordnance Survey) and then drawing our own map to show what something is like now. An example of this would be to show the location of new housing estates in a town that is growing in size.
- A choropleth map is a useful way to show how something varies across a map. It could show, for example, how the pedestrian density varies in different parts of a town:

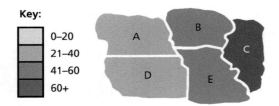

**Pedestrian density map
(number of people per hour)**

Key:

	0–20
	21–40
	41–60
	60+

> **Key Point**
>
> There are many different ways to present fieldwork data. It is important to choose the most appropriate method.

- If you have taken photos or made fieldwork sketches, these can be annotated with labels to present information about your topic:

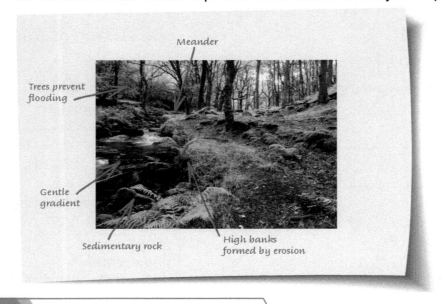

Meander

Trees prevent flooding

Gentle gradient

Sedimentary rock

High banks formed by erosion

- Much of the data that you want to present can be turned into different types of graphs. It is important to choose the right sort of graph:

Line graph
• If you are showing changes over time, then you need to draw a line graph. A good example would be to show how temperature changes over time at a particular place. If you wanted to compare two places, you could plot two lines on the same axes.

Bar chart
• If you are showing different amounts of something in different categories, then a bar chart would be a good choice. As an example you could show how the number of houses of each type (detached, semi-detached, terraced, bungalow) varied in a town.

- A pie chart is a useful method if you want to use percentages rather than raw data (original data). So for example, you could work out the percentage of people travelling to work by car/bus/walking/cycling and show this as a pie chart.
- Pictograms or picture graphs are an interesting way to present data. You need to decide on a symbol or picture to represent the amount, e.g. one stick person = 10 people. You can then, for example, draw the amount of stick people visiting different types of shop. You can also create a graph that uses symbols of different sizes.

Question: Do you enjoy living in your part of the town?
[30 people were asked in Area X and 30 people in Area Y]

Area X

Key: 1 cm wide face = 10 people

Area Y

Key Point

Presenting data helps us to understand the information that we have collected whilst working outside the classroom and draw conclusions.

Pie chart

Key Words

data
historical map
line graph
bar chart
raw data
pictogram

Quick Test

1. What do the letters OS mean?
2. What is a fieldwork sketch?
3. If 25 people walk to work and 75 people catch the bus, what percentage use public transport?
4. What is a pictogram?

Geographic Information Systems

1 What are the three things that you need for a Geographic Information System (GIS)? [3]

2 What, at a simple level, is a GIS used for? [1]

3 a) Why does the police service plot crime data on a GIS? [2]

   b) Name one other organisation that uses GIS. [1]

4 Why might you make a GIS layer transparent? [1]

5 a) What sort of information is shown as a point on a GIS layer? [1]

   b) What sort of information is shown as a line on a GIS layer? [1]

6 Read the following sentences and tick (✓) the ones that are true.

   A You cannot add data on most online GIS. ☐

   B You can add data on most online GIS. ☐

   C You can change data on most online GIS. ☐

   D You cannot change data on most online GIS. ☐ [2]

7 What sort of information might you find on an online local council GIS?
   Give two examples. [2]

8 a) What is Google Earth? [2]

   b) How can you learn about scale in Google Earth? [4]

9 a) What information can you see on a satellite image in Google Earth?
      Give two examples. [2]

   b) Complete the following sentence by filling in the missing words.

      As you zoom in from the global view in Google Earth, the satellite images are

      replaced by .... [1]

Fieldwork

1 **a)** What is another name for fieldwork? [1]

b) Draw lines to match each part of fieldwork with where it is normally carried out.

| Displaying data |

| Analysing data |

| Taking photos | | Outdoors |

| Conducting surveys | | In the classroom |

| Drawing conclusions | [5]

c) Why is the correct equipment, footwear and clothing important for successful fieldwork? [2]

2 Why must you be accurate when you collect data? [2]

3 Suggest two things that might be measured on a shopping study. [2]

4 What is a flow meter used for? [2]

5 Is the following question an open question or a closed question?

How many times a week do you walk to school?
1 ☐   2 ☐   3 ☐   4 ☐   5 ☐
[1]

6 Why might you use a historical map when presenting your fieldwork data? [2]

7 **a)** When would you use a bar chart to present fieldwork data? [2]

b) Why might you use a pictogram to show fieldwork data? [1]

Review Questions

Development

1 a) What term is used to describe developing countries?   [1]

     b) Give an example of a developing country.   [1]

2 What do social indicators measure?   [2]

3 Define life expectancy.   [2]

4 Give an example of a secondary industry.   [1]

5 What does NIC stand for? Tick (✓) the correct option.

    Newly independent country   ☐

    Northern industrialised country   ☐

    Newly industrialised country   ☐

    Newly independent company   ☐   [1]

6 Why are many LICs in debt?   [3]

7 Which of the following are Millennium Development Goals? Tick (✓) the
correct options.

    Child health   ☐

    Reduced child mortality   ☐

    Improved environment   ☐

    An end to poverty   ☐

    Greener transport   ☐

    Universal education   ☐   [4]

8 Define 'sustainable development'.   [3]

Economic Activity

1 Economic activities can be divided into three groups. Name the groups. [3]

2 What does the word 'manufacture' mean? [1]

3 **a)** What do farmers in LICs do with their surplus food? [2]

b) Where does the food grown on large farms in LICs usually end up? Give an example. [2]

4 **a)** Why do some farmers use large amounts of chemicals? [2]

b) What is the difference between an arable farm and a pastoral farm? [2]

5 Underline the correct word in the following sentence:

If work in a factory is mechanised, it is done by **hand/machines**. [1]

6 **a)** Name two products still made in factories in the UK. [2]

b) Which of the following products might be made in a high-tech factory? Tick (✓) the correct options.

A toy ☐

A book ☐

A smart phone ☐

A pizza ☐

A TV ☐ [2]

7 Which company is the world's largest mobile phone maker (by number of handsets sold)? Tick (✓) the correct option.

Apple ☐

Nokia ☐

Blackberry ☐

Samsung ☐ [1]

Review Questions

Natural Resources

1. What is special about renewable natural resources? [2]

2. What happens when we recycle natural resources? Give an example. [2]

3. The photo shows coniferous trees.

a) Are coniferous trees hardwood or softwood trees? [1]

b) How long does it take for a deciduous tree to reach full size? Tick (✓) the correct option.

10 years ☐   50 years ☐   over 100 years ☐ [1]

c) Why is it important that some of the rainforest trees are chopped down? [2]

4. a) Name two natural resources that humans collect from the sea. [2]

b) What effect does overfishing have on the natural resources in the sea? [2]

5. a) How much of our electricity in the UK comes from burning coal? Tick (✓) the correct option.

5% ☐   25% ☐   33% ☐   60% ☐ [1]

b) Why does burning coal cause problems for the environment? [2]

6. a) How important a fuel is oil in our power stations? [1]

b) Name two products made from oil that are used by farmers. [2]

Ordnance Survey Maps

1 Study this extract of the Landranger 1:50 000 Ordnance Survey Map.

a) Why do six-figure grid references give a more accurate location than four-figure grid references? [4]

b) Give six-figure grid references for:

i) the public house south of Rejarrah Farm on the A3075 [2]

ii) the T-junction in Goonhavern of the B3285 with the A3075. [2]

c) What is found at the following grid references? [2]

   i) 786577 [2]

   ii) 785542 [2]

   iii) 811617 [2]

d) Locate square 8355 and give the six-figure reference for the following:

   i) the big building in the top NW corner of the square [2]

   ii) the golf course [2]

   iii) the deciduous forest in the SW corner of the square. [2]

Geographic Information Systems

1 How does a GIS help the ambulance service? [1]

2 a) In a GIS, what does a layer show? Give an example. [2]

b) Why might you switch layers on or off? [2]

c) What is usually used as the base layer in a GIS? Tick (✓) the correct option.

A quadrat ☐

A graph ☐

A map ☐ [1]

d) Name one other type of information that could be used as a base layer. [1]

3 What sort of information is shown as a polygon on a GIS layer? [1]

4 Why is text needed on a GIS layer? [1]

5 What does a Google Earth tour do? [2]

Fieldwork

1 a) Where might you carry out local fieldwork? Tick (✓) the correct options.

France ☐

In another country ☐

In the school grounds ☐

In the local neighbourhood ☐ [2]

b) Which part of the fieldwork process is carried out 'in the field'? [1]

2 Why is health and safety important for successful fieldwork? [1]

3 What is a georeferenced photo? [2]

4 Describe two things that might be measured on a beach study. [2]

5 a) What is an anonymous questionnaire? [1]

b) Give an example of an open question that could be used on a questionnaire. [2]

6 What is the name given to this type of map? [1]

Increase in tonnes per annum
☐ 0–20
☐ 21–40
☐ 41–60
☐ 61–80
■ 81–100
■ 101–120
■ >120

7 Look at the data in the table.

People Visiting Different Kinds of Shops			
Food	Clothes shop	Phone shop	Sports shop
120	46	24	10

a) Change this raw data into percentages. [4]

b) Draw a pie chart to display the data. [4]

Mixed Test-Style Questions

1 **a)** Explain why individuals and companies carry out economic activities.

....

....

....

....

2 marks

b) Describe the kind of work done by people working in primary activities.

....

....

....

3 marks

c) State whether each of the following sentences is **true** or **false**.

i) In HICs, 70–80% of people work in the tertiary sector. ....

ii) In HICs, a large percentage of people work in the primary sector. ....

iii) In LICs such as Nigeria, most people work in the tertiary sector. ....

3 marks

2 Name the countries from their outlines. (*Not to scale*).

a)   **b)**   **c)**

a) ....

b) ....

c) ....

3 marks

3　a) List three similarities between South Korea in 1953 and Kenya today.

　　i) ....

　　ii) ....

　　iii) ....

☐ 3 marks

　b) Describe what it is like to live in South Korea today.

....

....

....

☐ 3 marks

4　a) Name three processes of erosion that take place in rivers.

　　i) ....

　　ii) ....

　　iii) ....

☐ 3 marks

　b) The photos show landforms found at different stages of rivers.

　　Underneath each one, write **upper**, **middle** or **lower** to show where each is found.

i)

Meander

ii)

Waterfall

iii)

Floodplain

....　　......................................　　......................................

☐ 3 marks

TOTAL

☐
23

Mixed Test-Style Questions

5 Explain, with examples, the difference between renewable and non-renewable resources.

....

....

....

....

....

....

5 marks

6 Describe the arguments for and against cutting timber from tropical rainforests.

....

....

....

....

4 marks

7 **a)** Name the three main rivers in the Middle East.

i) ....   ii) ....

iii) ....

3 marks

b) Explain why major cities in the Middle East are often located close to rivers.

....

....

2 marks

c) Which other natural resource has influenced economic development in the Middle East and why hasn't every country in the Middle East benefited from this?

....

....

2 marks

8 a) Match the letter of each rock with the named rocks below.

A

B

C

Granite ....

Sandstone ....

Chalk ....

3 marks

b) Granite is an igneous rock. Describe the characteristics of igneous rocks.

....

....

....

3 marks

9 Define the term 'urbanisation'.

....

....

2 marks

10 How can a country's level of development be measured?

....

....

3 marks

11 Draw a graph with labelled axes to show how world population has grown over the last 100 years and add some annotations.

6 marks

TOTAL

33

Mixed Test-Style Questions

12 Explain, with examples, why few people choose to live in difficult environments.

_____

_____

_____

_____

_____

4 marks

13 a) Name a **cold** desert and a **hot** desert.

1) Cold desert _____

2) Hot desert _____

2 marks

b) Describe the similarities and differences between hot deserts and cold deserts.

_____

_____

_____

_____

4 marks

14 Which of the following are examples of fragile landscapes? Tick (✓) the correct options.

4 marks

Tropical rainforests ☐   Deciduous woodlands ☐

Deserts ☐   Savannah grasslands ☐

15 a) Explain how mountains are formed when crustal plates move.

2 marks

_____

_____

_____

_____

3 marks

b) Look at the diagram. What type of plate boundary is shown?

....

☐

1 mark

16 **a)** Study the photograph below. Name the type of weathering that is shown.

....

☐

1 mark

b) Draw lines to match each statement to the type of weathering it describes.

Happens in cold, mountainous areas	Biological weathering
Often occurs in deserts due to the temperature change	Freeze-thaw weathering
Takes place when weak acid in rainwater dissolves rocks	Chemical weathering
Occurs when plants and animals break down rocks	Onion-skin weathering

☐

4 marks

TOTAL

☐

21

Mixed Test-Style Questions

17 **a)** Explain how a glacier can shape the landscape.

_____

_____

_____

_____

☐ 4 marks

b) Name one glacial landform that results from deposition.

_____

☐ 1 mark

18 Why have many city centres experienced decline over time?

_____

_____

_____

_____

☐ 3 marks

19 Describe the difference between each type of precipitation.

_____

_____

_____

_____

☐ 4 marks

20 How would we measure the two different wind elements at a weather station?

_____

_____

_____

☐ 4 marks

21 Study the graph below showing the effect of angle of slope and land use on soil erosion.

a) Which land use creates the most soil erosion?

....

1 mark

b) Explain why less soil erosion takes place where the land use is forest.

....

....

....

....

4 marks

c) Which of the following are ways that farmers can reduce the amount of soil erosion from their fields?

Tick (✓) the correct options.

Cattle grazing ☐

Contour ploughing ☐

Building terraced fields ☐

Building dry-stone walls ☐

Planting trees ☐

3 marks

TOTAL

☐

24

Mixed Test-Style Questions

22 Describe three ways that Kenya is connected to the UK.

i) ....

....

ii) ....

....

iii) ....

....

☐ 3 marks

23 **a)** Why are fossils an important part of the Geological Timescale?

....

....

....

....

☐ 3 marks

b) Place the following creatures into the flowchart to show the order in which they appeared on Earth.

Humans   Fish   Dinosaurs   Birds

Earliest ☐ ⟶ ☐ ⟶ ☐ ⟶ ☐ **Latest**   ☐ 4 marks

24 What happens to the Earth when it becomes glaciated?

....

....

....

....

☐ 4 marks

25 The photograph shows a favela in Sao Paulo, Brazil. Explain why shanty towns might develop in LICs.

....

....

....

....

5 marks

26 **a)** Explain why you might collect data when doing fieldwork.

....

....

....

4 marks

b) What sort of annotations might you add to a fieldwork photo taken in the high street of a town centre?

....

....

....

4 marks

TOTAL

27

Mixed Test-Style Questions

27 What equipment might you need for a microclimate study in the school grounds? What would you record?

_____

_____

_____

_____

_____

[ ]

4 marks

28 **a)** Which of the following are examples of hard engineering? Tick (✓) the correct options.

Building dams [ ]   Restricting building on flood plains [ ]

Giving flood warnings [ ]   Creating reservoirs [ ]

[ ]

2 marks

b) Using examples, outline the advantages and disadvantages of hard and soft engineering on the coast.

_____

_____

_____

_____

[ ]

4 marks

29 **a)** Explain with an example why a GIS is a useful tool.

_____

_____

_____

_____

[ ]

4 marks

b) Why doesn't it matter how many layers you have in a GIS?

....

....

....

....

2 marks

c) Explain the difference between a line and a point in a GIS.

....

....

....

....

4 marks

30 Imagine you are a farmer who lives in a post-glaciated landscape. Write a letter to the council explaining your concerns about the increasing tourist numbers.

Dear Sir/Madam

....

....

....

....

....

....

....

5 marks

TOTAL

25

Mixed Test-Style Questions

31 Explain, with examples, why many of the goods we buy are made in LICs or NICs.

_____

_____

_____

_____

2 marks

32 Why in general are earthquakes more dangerous than volcanoes?

_____

_____

_____

_____

3 marks

33 What are the similarities and differences between tropical climates and desert climates?

_____

_____

_____

_____

3 marks

TOTAL

8

Answers

Page 5 Quick Test
1. Taiga. **2.** Permafrost. **3.** The Volga. **4.** 5 million people.

Page 7 Quick Test
1. Rice, tea, wheat, cotton, peanuts, tobacco. (Any three)
2. 400 million. **3.** Yangtse; 6300 km. **4.** The Communist Party.

Page 9 Quick Test
1. Alpine tundra. **2.** July to September. **3.** The Indus.
4. 1947.

Page 11 Quick Test
1. 2.3 million km^2 **2.** It is the largest sand desert in the world.
3. Arab. **4.** Islam, Christianity (or other suitable answer).

Page 13 Quick Test
1. 582 650 km^2 **2.** Between January and March. **3.** Nairobi.

Page 15 Quick Test
1. 30%. **2.** Temperate monsoon. **3.** 48 million.

Page 17 Quick Test
1. 4.6 billion years old. **2.** Charles Darwin. **3.** North Wales and north-west Scotland. **4.** 160 million years.

Page 19 Quick Test
1. There was no atmosphere. **2.** As an adaptation to extreme cold. **3.** Factories and vehicles. **4.** A few centimetres per year.

Page 21 Quick Test
1. The core. **2.** Plates. **3.** South America. **4.** 1906.

Page 23 Quick Test
1. Very common – thousands may occur every day.
2. The focus is where an earthquake starts.
3. Due to the ground cracking and gas pipes breaking.
4. The molten rock that comes out of a volcano.

Key Concepts from Key Stage 2
1. **a)** Equator – C; Tropic of Capricorn – D; Tropic of Cancer – B; Greenwich Meridian – A **[4]**
   b) i) Brazil – Yellow; ii) Argentina – Blue;
   iii) Italy – Red; iv) USA – Orange;
   v) Sweden – Blue **[5]**
2. **a)** i) Richter scale **[1]** ii) Epicentre **[1]**
   iii) Extinct **[1]**
   b) i) A – Source; B – Tributary; C – Confluence;
   D – Mouth; E – Watershed **[5]**
   ii) evaporation; condensation; precipitation; run-off; groundwater **[5]**
3. **a)** Primary activity – Farmer; Secondary activity – Metal worker; Tertiary activity – Dentist **[3]**
   b) i) cities **[1]** ii) hamlet **[1]** iii) conurbation **[1]**

Page 26: Location Knowledge – Russia, China, India and the Middle East
1. **a)** It has fertile soil **[1]** called chernozem. **[1]**
   b) 100°C **[1]** 250 mm **[1]**
2. **a)** i) Moscow **[1]**
   ii) 11 million **[1]**
   b) Death rates **[1]** are rising **[1]** and people are having fewer children **[1]** due to economic uncertainty **[1]**

3. People can own and run their own businesses **[1]**; the government has encouraged international trade **[1]**
4. It has hot wet summers, **[1]** cold dry winters **[1]** and fertile land from river sediments. **[1]**
5. **a)** A small percentage increase will have a dramatic effect on India's already large population. **[1]** Increasing wealth may encourage people to have more children (although often family size decreases when a country becomes richer). **[1]** Some religions do not condone contraception. **[1]**
   b) India has such a large population that its GDP per capita is small. **[1]** Inequality means that the majority of the wealth in concentrated into the hands of a minority. **[1]**
6. He campaigned for independence for India **[1]** from the British Empire **[1]** and was the first prime minister **[1]** of an independent India. **[1]**
7. **a)** 4.13 million km^2 **[1]**
   b) Europe **[1]** Africa **[1]** Asia **[1]**
8. It connects the Mediterranean Sea to the Red Sea **[1]** allowing sea transport between Europe and Asia **[1]** without having to go around Africa. **[1]**

Page 27: Africa and Asia Compared – Kenya and South Korea
1. **a)** Western Kenya **[1]**
   b) It is formed by the African plate **[1]** stretching and slowly tearing apart, **[1]** so the land is sinking downwards. **[1]**
2. Coffee **[1]** Tea **[1]** Flowers **[1]**
3. Kenya is a poor country. **[1]** It does not have the resources to cope with rapid population growth **[1]** and struggles to provide housing, jobs, education and healthcare. **[1]**
4. **a)** 200 000 **[1]** safari **[1]** Mombasa **[1]**
   b) Tourism provides jobs for 800 000 Kenyans **[1]** It is a source of foreign money for the country, **[1]** providing 22% of Kenya's export earnings. **[1]**
5. A large South Korean company **[1]** that produces a wide range of goods and services. **[1]**
6. **a)** Built new roads; **[1]** took control of factories; **[1]** built steel works; **[1]** concentrated on manufacturing industry; **[1]** built new schools; **[1]** kept wages low. **[1]**
   b) It grew from $872 **[1]** to $7455 **[1]**
7. South Korea's longest river is the Nakdong River **[1]** A free trade agreement exists between the EU and South Korea **[1]**
8. **a)** 2012 **[1]**
   b) 19 people were killed **[1]** 1.9 million homes lost power **[1]** $374 million damage. **[1]**

Page 28: Geological Timescale
1. **a)** The Geological Timescale shows the history of the Earth related to different rock types **[1]** and the fossils associated with them. **[1]**
   b) 1 billion years after the Earth was first formed. **[1]**
   c) A fossil is the remains of a plant or animal **[1]** trapped in the rocks. **[1]**
2. Dinosaurs. **[1]**
3. The group of apes that humans belong to. **[1]**
4. It didn't rain when the Earth was first formed as there was no atmosphere. **[1]**
5. **a)** During the last glaciation humans moved south **[1]** to where it was warmer **[1]**
   b) During a glaciation, the sea level falls **[1]** as the water is trapped on land as ice **[1]**
6. Greenhouse gases trap heat in the atmosphere **[1]** The climate becomes warmer **[1]**

Page 29: Plate Tectonics
1. **a)** A – Core **[1]** B – Mantle **[1]** C – Crust **[1]**
   b) Because it is relatively thin when compared to the overall size of the Earth. **[1]**
   c) It causes the rocks in the mantle to become soft **[1]** and they slowly flow. **[1]**

2. Pangaea [1]
3. a) An earthquake is a violent shaking of the ground where tectonic plates are moving alongside each other. [1]
   b) Most damage is caused at the epicentre [1] as this is the point on the surface directly above the focus of the earthquake. [1]
4. Waves up to 30 m (100 ft) high [1] killed large numbers of people living along the coast. [1]
5. International aid is help or money given by countries to help people who have suffered a natural disaster such as an earthquake [1], e.g. medical supplies or rescue teams [1].
6. Volcanoes in Hawaii are low and wide [1] Land near volcanoes is fertile [1]

Pages 31–45 Revise Questions

Page 31 Quick Test
1. Porous   2.   Erosion, transportation, deposition, lithification
3. Lava   4.   Igneous

Page 33 Quick Test
1. Rainfall, temperature and atmospheric gases   2.   It freezes and expands   3.   Oxygen and water   4.   The tree puts roots through joints and cracks in the rocks causing them to split open.

Page 35 Quick Test
1. The breakdown of rocks by the action of the weather, plants and animals.
2. Hot during the day and cold at night.

Page 37 Quick Test
1. Humus.   2.   Nutrients, minerals and humus.   3.   20–30 metres.

Page 39 Quick Test
1. Weather is the daily changes in the atmospheric conditions.
2. Precipitation is another name for rainfall.
3. An anemometer measures wind speed.

Page 41 Quick Test
1. Temperature and rainfall.   2.   Between the Tropics of Cancer and Capricorn.   3.   A desert climate.   4.   The height of the land.

Page 43 Quick Test
1. Plucking and abrasion.   2.   Firn forms when accumulated snow begins to become compacted and dense.   3.   Bowl shaped/armchair shaped/steep back wall and lip at the front.   4.   The main valley glacier cuts off smaller glaciers leaving the smaller valleys hanging above the main valley.

Page 45 Quick Test
1. Egg or teardrop shaped with a tapered end downstream.
2. They are transported over long distances from their origins.
3. Footpath erosion, noise/water pollution from speedboats, dog walkers disturb sheep, traffic jams. (Any two)

Pages 46–49 Review Questions

Page 46: Location Knowledge – Russia, China, India and the Middle East
1. –50°C. [1]
2. a) Materials that are found in the natural environment [1] that are useful to people. [1]
   b) Information technology [1], nanotechnology [1], space industry. [1]
3. Beijing, [1] 19.6 million. [1]
4. a) 12th May [1] 2008. [1]
   b) 8. [1]
   c) 87 000. [1]
5. 700 000 km². [1]
6. Hindu. [1]

7. Any four: motor vehicles, [1] shipbuilding, [1] chemicals, [1] telecommunications, [1] computers, [1] software. [1]
8. a) Arabian, [1] Sahara. [1]
   b) 650 000 km² [1] 250 m. [1]
9. Qatar, [1] Bahrain, [1] Kuwait, [1] Oman. [1]

Page 47: Africa and Asia Compared – Kenya and South Korea
1. Two times larger.
2. 1390 mm, [1] similar to the UK. [1]
3. A type of tropical rainforest found in upland areas [1] where there is very high humidity. [1]
4. Mt Hallasan, [1] 1950 metres. [1]
5. Oak, birch, spruce, yew. (Any three for [3])
6. 79 years. [1]
7. a) 1945, [1] Japan. [1]
   b) 3 million. [1]

Page 48: Geological Timescale
1. Sedimentary rocks. [1]
2. a) Precambrian rocks. [1]
   b) North Wales and north-west Scotland. [1]
3. The creatures that survive are those that are best adapted [1] to their environment. [1]
4. The dinosaurs became extinct when an asteroid [1] struck the Earth. [1]
5. a) Africa. [1]
   b) Modern-day humans. [1]
   c) The brains of modern-day humans are much larger than those of their ancestors. [1]
6. If we are in an inter-glacial [1] and an ice age returns. [1]
7. a) The chalk in south-east England formed from sediments deposited in a warm, tropical sea [1] when the UK was located much further south than now. [1]
   b) The UK once had a desert climate [1] many millions of years ago. [1]

Page 49: Plate Tectonics
1. a) Where two plates meet. [1]
   b) Examples: Alps in Europe, Himalayas in Asia, Andes in South America, Rocky Mountains in North America. [1]
   c) When two plates move apart at a constructive plate boundary, molten magma [1] from the mantle [1] fills the gap.
2. The UK and the USA are on different plates [1] and the two plates are moving very slowly apart. [1]
3. a) A tsunami is a large wave [1] caused by underwater earthquakes [1] which shake the sea bed. [1]
   b) Damage to buildings, roads, railways, bridges, underground pipes and cables can be caused. (Two examples for [2])
   c) Many people may die after an earthquake due to injuries [1] or a lack of food and water. [1]
4. A hot spot is a weakness in the Earth's crust [1] where molten rock can escape. [1]
5. a) Two plates meet here [1] and molten rock escapes to form volcanoes. [1]
   b) The soil is very fertile [1] and good for growing crops. [1]

Pages 50–53 Practice Questions

Page 50: Rocks and Geology
1. a) Igneous rocks are formed when magma cools [1] and solidifies. [1]
   b) If magma cools slowly the rock will have large crystals; [2] if magma cools quickly the rock will have small crystals. [2]
2. a) 28%. [1]
   b) limestone = marble, [1] shale = slate. [1]
3. Sedimentary rocks [1] are most likely because the remains of plants and animals become trapped between layers of sediment. [1]
4. You can clearly see the layers in the rock, [1] which show that it was formed from layers of sediment over millions of years. [1]

Page 51: Weathering and Soil

1. a) Cold mountainous environments. [1]
    b) A — 2 [1]
        B — 3 [1]
        C — 1 [1]
2. Plant roots [1] and animal burrows [1] can break up and destroy rock.
3. a) climate = high temperatures increase the rate of soil formation; [1] organisms = insects, worms and plants; [1] parent material = the type of rock that the soil has weathered from; [1] relief = the shape of the land. [1]
    b) Time. [1]
4. 75 billion tonnes [1]
5. Latosol. [1]

Page 52: Weather and Climate

1. Humidity [1] wind [1]
2. Minimum temperature = Lowest temperature recorded each day; Humidity = Amount of moisture in the air; Precipitation = Amount of moisture that reaches the ground. [3]
3. Hail is a pellet of ice falling from a cloud. [1]
4. It will increase the air pressure. [1]
5. Examples: farmer, fisherman, construction worker, driver, etc. plus a logical reason for the choice, e.g. a farmer would use the weather forecast to help decide when to sow seeds (Any example with explanation for [2]).
6. When air is warmed by the sun, it rises. [1]
7. A = Temperature [1] B = Rainfall [1].
8. Either side of the equator between the Tropic of Cancer [1] and the Tropic of Capricorn [1].
9. The Gulf Stream is a warm ocean current [1] that flows from the Gulf of Mexico [1] towards the UK. [1]

Page 53: Glaciation

1. a) A large moving body of ice [1] that flows slowly down a valley due to the force of gravity. [1]
    b) The last glacial period. [1]
    c) When more snow falls than can melt, the snow builds up: accumulation [1]; over time, the weight of the snow causes it to become compacted and dense; [1] at this stage it is called firn; [1] the weight of the ice mass causes it to slide and advance downhill [1] due to gravity. [1]
2. Freeze-thaw; [1] plucking; [1] abrasion. [1]
3. A = lateral; [1] B = medial; [1] C = terminal. [1]
4. a) an obstruction; [1] b) deposited; [1] c) streamlines; [1]
    d) advancing. [1]
5. Footpaths may become overused [1] meaning vegetation is destroyed and land is eroded. [1] Speedboats [1] may lead to noise and water pollution. [1] Tourists may not be aware of farming practices [1] and their dogs could disturb livestock [1] (Three impacts clearly explained for [6].)

Pages 55–69 Revise Questions

Page 55 Quick Test

1. Attrition, corrasion/abrasion, hydraulic action, solution. 2. The act of depositing a sediment. 3. Deposition.

Page 57 Quick Test

1. Waves and weather. 2. The wind. 3. Longshore drift.
4. Tourists/environmentalists.

Page 59 Quick Test

1. Growing populations need land and resources. 2. Trees absorb carbon dioxide from the atmosphere. 3. Between forest and desert environmental regions. 4. The process by which land becomes infertile and unproductive desert.

Page 61 Quick Test

1. They find food, clothing, and housing from the forest. 2. They know how to live a sustainable existence and can inform management strategies based on this knowledge. 3. Replacing trees that have been cut down. 4. Circles of stones placed on the ground to prevent water runoff.

Page 63 Quick Test

1. 80 million people. 2. There will not be enough resources for all the extra people. 3. These areas do not have the resources that people need. 4. Western Europe has the resources that people need to survive and have a good quality of life – water, flat land, fertile soil, minerals.

Page 65 Quick Test

1. Emigrants leave a country and immigrants arrive in a country.
2. Refugees have lost their homes due to different kinds of disasters. 3. UK: 12.3 (BR) – 9.3 (DR) = 3.0   India: 20.9 (BR) – 7.5 (DR) = 13.4 4. People eat lots of 'junk food' and do not exercise enough.

Page 67 Quick Test

1. The process by which the proportion of people living in urban areas grows.
2. People are pushed from rural areas by lack of jobs/good healthcare/education and pulled to the cities by the attraction of opportunities for work/education, resulting in growth of towns and cities and decline of rural areas.
3. People move out from city centres to avoid pollution and overcrowding.
4. Following economic/social and environmental decline as people and jobs moved away from cities.

Page 69 Quick Test

1. In HICs urbanisation occurred at a steady rate, in LICs it has happened more rapidly.
2. Makeshift housing on unwanted land around the city.
3. When local people are involved in the planning/management process.
4. Social, economic and environmental factors.

Pages 70–73 Review Questions

Page 70: Rocks and Geology

1. Rock that can absorb water. [1]
2. a) i) Older rocks [1] and the remains of living organisms. [1]
        ii) Any three from: chalk, [1] limestone, [1] sandstone, [1] shale, [1] clay, [1] coal, [1] conglomerate, [1] breccia. [1]
    b) i) Heat [1] and pressure. [1]
        ii) Any three from: marble, [1] slate, [1] schist, [1] gneiss. [1]
3. Intrusive rocks are igneous rocks that have formed from magma that has solidified inside the Earth [1] whereas extrusive rocks are igneous rocks that have formed from magma that has solidified on the surface of the Earth. [1]
4. A = Eroded particles transported by rivers to the sea. [1] B = Particles sink to the bottom of the sea. [1] C = Particles build up in layers. [1] D = Over millions of years new rock forms on the seabed. [1]
5. Igneous rocks are formed from molten rock beneath the Earth's surface [1], known as magma [1]. This includes rocks made from lava from volcanic eruptions [1] or rocks made from solidified magma underground [1].

Page 71: Weathering and Soil

1. Calcium carbonate, [1] carbonic acid. [1]
2. 1 - Water gets into cracks in rocks, [1] 2 - water freezes and expands, [1] 3 - rocks split and break up. [1]
3. Changes in temperature cause the surface of the rock to expand and contract [1] because it is exposed to the direct heat of the sun/cooling effect of the night; [1] this creates stress between the surface of the rock and its core [1] because they are expanding and contracting at different rates. [1]
4. Weathering is the breakdown of rocks by the action of plants, animals and the weather; [1] erosion is the removal of weathered material by the action of wind or water. [1]
5. a) 75 bn tonnes. [1]
    b) Because it can take hundreds of years for soil to form. [1]

c) Any three from: type of soil, [1] angle of slope, [1] strength of the wind, [1] water flowing over the surface, [1] vegetation cover. [1]
6. 1–2 m deep, [1] thick topsoil (20 cm), [1] took 10 000 years to form. [1]
7. a) 45 % [1]
    b) 10 000 years [1]

Page 72: Weather and Climate
1. Hail [1] and snow. [1]
2. a) The wind may bring warm or cold air depending where it comes from. [1]
    b) High wind speeds can cause damage to trees and buildings. [1]
3. South-east England. [1]
4. On a foggy day humidity will be high. [1]
5. A weather forecast for the next 24 hours [1] as it is difficult to predict the weather a long way into the future. [1]
6. The UK has average temperatures of around 5°C in winter [1] and around 17°C in summer [1] so the difference is about 12°C. [1]
7. a) Polar, temperate, desert, tropical. (One mark per correct answer.) [4]
    b) The temperature would be hot all year round [1] with a high total rainfall. [1]
8. The sun strikes the Earth at a low angle near the poles [1] and is reflected back into space. [1]

Page 73: Glaciation
1. Snow builds up [1] when more snow falls than can melt. [1]
2. When melting [1] is greater than accumulation. [1]
3. Ribbon lake. [1]
4. In a corrie [1] after the glacier has melted. [1]
5. A = pyramidal peak [1]; B = hanging valley [1]; C = U-shaped valley [1]
6. The material deposited [1] on a valley floor after a glacier melts. [1]
7. Look out of place [1] because they usually have a completely different rock type [1] from those in the locations where they are dropped.
8. A beautiful/scenic area/landscape [1] that attracts large numbers of tourists [1] during seasonal months. [1]
9. a) Farmers; [1] environmentalists; [1] tourists; [1] local councils; [1] residents. [1] (Any three groups for [3].)
    b) They may forget to keep dogs on leads [1] which means livestock may be harmed; [1] may overuse footpaths [1] and cause soil erosion and the destruction of vegetation. [1]
    c) They can educate the tourists about the landscape; [1] provide information [1] to inform tourists on which paths to use to avoid overuse; [1] or how to behave around farmland areas. [1]

Pages 74–77 Practice Questions

Page 74: Rivers and Coasts
1. Erosion; [1] transportation; [1] deposition. [1]
2. Rocks carried within the water [1] erode the riverbed and banks. [1]
3. Waterfall; V-shaped valley; rapids; gorge. (Any one for [1])
4. Meander; [1] A = deposition; [1] B = erosion. [1]
5. A river will flood when water reaches the channel faster than it can be carried downstream. [1] Overland flow can lead to flooding as this is the fastest route to the channel. [1]
6. Wind blows over the surface of the sea; [1] oscillations are caused by friction between wind and sea; [1] wave energy is transferred forward in the direction of the prevailing wind; [1] wave height increases due to friction between sea and seabed; [1] top of wave moves faster than bottom. [1]
7. A = wave-cut notch; [1] B = wave-cut platform. [1]
8. Advantages: immediate/effective coastal protection; [1] groynes prevent longshore drift and create wide beaches. [1]

Disadvantages: can be expensive to maintain; [1] can be an eyesore; [1] can limit access to the beach. [1] (One advantage and one disadvantage for [2])

Page 75: Landscapes
1. A growing population [1] means that towns and cities are increasing in size. [1]
2. Over 7 billion [1].
3. Removing trees and vegetation [1] to make space for farming and cities [1]; digging mines and quarries [1] for natural resources [1]; controlling rivers [1] for electricity. [1] (Any three for [3])
4. Amazon rainforest; [1] 370 billion trees; [1] Trees act as a carbon sink for CO_2 emissions. [1]
5. a) They find food, clothing, and housing from the forest [1] so do not require manufactured goods/fuel [1]; move their villages regularly [1] to allow the landscape to recover and grow back [1]; live a sustainable existence [1] because they use the land without destroying the environment. [1] (Points must be explained for [4].)
    b) Populations are decreasing because many have died from introduced diseases such as measles [1]; been forced into cities [1]; had their environment destroyed by deforestation [1].
    c) By working with indigenous people, we can learn important information about rainforests — their ecology, [1] medicinal plants, [1] food and other products [1]; people can teach [1] valuable lessons about managing rainforests sustainably. [1]
6. Conservation of savannah landscapes [1] can protect them from desertification because areas are protected from over grazing/over cultivation [1]; trees are planted [1] to protect soils and prevent soil erosion [1]; Terracing [1] means soil is not washed down the slope when it rains [1]

Page 76: Population
1. a) Almost 7.5 billion people. [1]
    b) In the past population growth was low [1] but now it is very fast. [1]
    c) Over 10 billion. [1]
2. In a sparse population, there are few people [1] whereas in a dense population, there are many people. [1]
3. Although Alaska has a very cold climate, [1] it has many resources such as oil that attract people. [1]
4. High population density examples: Bangladesh, South Korea; [1] low population density examples: Peru, Russia. [1]
5. An illegal immigrant does not have permission to enter a country and may be asked to leave [1] whereas a refugee has lost their home and has special permission to seek help in another country. [1]
6. If the birth rate is higher than the death rate, then there will be a natural increase in the population. [1]
7. A family planning campaign aims to reduce [1] the number of babies being born. [1]
8. Too many older people who require lots of expensive care. [1] Too few people of working age so not enough people to do the jobs. [1]

Page 77: Urbanisation
1. a) The process by which the proportion of people living in urban areas grows; [1] more people live and work in towns and cities than remain in the countryside. [1]
    b) Rural to urban migration [1] means people migrate from the countryside to the cities; [1] natural increase [1] means more births than deaths. [1]
    c) More machines like tractors means fewer people are needed to work; [1] this means fewer jobs in rural areas; [1] people move to cities to find employment. [1]
2. Suburbanisation is the growth of urban areas around a city centre; [1] counterurbanisation is the growth of smaller villages and towns [1] beyond the main urban area. [1]

3. a) People moving away from cities; [1] industry moving away from cities; [1] means that inner cities are declining economically, [1] socially and environmentally. [1]
    b) Aim to attract people [1] and businesses back to city centres; [1] for example the London Docklands Development Corporation [1] was set up in 1981 to attract new businesses; money and people back to the area. [1]
4. Unlike the steady growth of HIC cities over 200 years [1] LIC cities have grown rapidly in just 60 years. [1]
5. a) Corrugated iron roofs; [1] no electricity; [1] no waste disposal; [1] lack of roads. [1]
    b) Local people [1] are granted ownership of their land [1] and provided with training [1] and tools to improve the homes themselves. [1]
6. Six appropriate characteristics identified:
    Walking and cycling is safe – pedestrianised streets [1]
    Recycling bins [1]
    Open green spaces [1]
    Traffic calming in roads [1]
    Bus and bike lanes [1]
    Street lighting makes cities safer [1]
    Energy efficient homes (e.g. with solar panels/well insulated) [1]

Pages 79–93 Revise Questions

Page 79 Quick Test
1. Varying economic, social, technological and cultural levels of development across the world.
2. Examples include: life expectancy; infant mortality rates; literacy rates.
3. They spend more on their imports than they make on their exports.
4. An imaginary line on the world map dividing the wealthy north from the poor south.

Page 81 Quick Test
1. Development measures that combine a variety of indicators to examine the economic, social and cultural characteristics of a country.
2. GDP can be high, but social development may still be low.
3. Is often tied to conditions unfavourable to the LIC; can cause LICs to become dependent on aid and can lead to huge debts.
4. Development that meets the needs of the present generation without compromising the ability of future generations to meet their own needs.

Page 83 Quick Test
1. People carry out economic activities to earn money.
2. Nursing is a tertiary or service activity.   3.   A food surplus is 'spare food' not needed by the farmer.   4.   Farmers grow cotton to sell to make cloth.

Page 85 Quick Test
1. To get their products to market and import raw materials.   2.   Newly Industrialising Country.   3.   Possible examples include computers, smart phones and TVs.
    4.   Very important – most jobs in the UK (around 75%) are service jobs.

Page 87 Quick Test
1. Natural resources are created by nature.   2.   They provide the food, materials and energy we need to survive.   3.   Examples include: wood, fish, minerals, etc.   4.   No – many are non-renewable, many of them will run out.

Page 89 Quick Test
1. Fish.   2.   Coal.   3.   Electricity.   4.   An import is a product bought from another country.

Page 91 Quick Test
1. North   2.   2 cm by 2 cm   3.   1 km^2

Page 93 Quick Test
1. 10   2.   10 metres   3.   Blue   4.   Public house

Pages 94–97 Review Questions

Page 94: Rivers and Coasts
1. Upper; middle; lower. [3]
2. a) Attrition; corrasion or abrasion; hydraulic action; solution. [4]
    b) Waterfall (or any other landform where erosion is the dominant process, e.g. potholes; rapids). [1]
    c) Floodplains or levees. [1]
3. Saturated soils; heavy rain; impermeable rock = physical cause. [3]
    Urbanisation and deforestation = Human cause. [2]
4. Different types of rock [1] will erode at different rates due to variations in resistance/strength. [1]   *Weather?*
5. Swash is more powerful than backwash in constructive waves. [1] Backwash is more powerful than swash in destructive waves. [1]
6. Soft rock – Sandstone [1]; hard rock – chalk, granite [2].
7. Longshore drift. [1]
8. Residents and tourists. [1] Residents may wish to use hard engineering to protect their homes and businesses effectively and immediately. [1] Tourists may disagree because hard engineering, such as sea walls, can limit their enjoyment of the area. [1]

Page 95: Landscapes
1. a) To use the world's resources [1] for your own gain/benefit [1]
    b) Cutting down trees/deforestation [1]; digging mines/quarries for coal [1]; controlling rivers for electricity [1] (Any two for [2])
2. The demand for space grows [1] and demand for resources grows [1], more fragile landscapes are exploited [1]; land cannot support growing populations [1] unsustainable [1] (Any three for [3])
3. a) Carbon dioxide [1]
    b) It is a greenhouse gas [1]
4. a) Increased dry periods [1] and less rainfall [1]
    b) Infertile [1] and unproductive [1]
5. a) Soil is unprotected from heavy rain [1] meaning it is washed away/eroded [1]
    b) Trees protect the soil from heavy rain [1] and roots bind the soil together [1]
6. a) Increased demand for space, fuel, resources found in rainforests. (Any two for [2])
    b) Originating and living/occurring naturally [1] in an area or environment [1]
    c) Can teach valuable lessons about how to manage these areas sustainably [1]; hold important information about ecology/medicinal plants [1]; are ancient peoples that have the right to live in their ancestral land [1]

Page 96: Population
1. a) The global birth rate is more than double the global death rate [1] so there are lots of extra people per year. [1]
    b) As the birth rate is falling in almost every country, [1] eventually the birth rate and the death rate will be the same [1] and so the world population will stop growing. [1]
2. Examples: Sahara Desert – too dry, Himalayas – too mountainous, Antarctica – too cold. (Any two plus reason for [4])
3. London [1] has the highest population density (5000 people per square kilometre) compared to the Highlands (10 people per square kilometre). [1]
4. In a civil war, families would leave their homes and flee to another country [1] to be safe from the fighting. [1]
5. Falling. [1]
6. Many HICs have high death rates as unhealthy lifestyles [1] lead to high rates of obesity, cancer and heart disease ([1] for an example).

Answers 135

7. Many migrants from Eastern Europe are coming to live in the UK because they are allowed to travel freely within Europe [1] and there are often better paid jobs in the UK. [1]

Page 97: Urbanisation
1. a) High Income Country; [1] Low Income Country. [1]
   b) Low Income Countries. [1]
2. a) As technology and transport improves [1] people begin to move away from cities to live [1] and work. [1]
   b) Suburbanisation [1] and counterurbanisation. [1]
3. a) Crime; abandoned shops; derelict factories. [3]
   b) A process aimed at attracting people [1] and businesses back to city centres [1]; Example: derelict factories are converted into flats and offices. [1]
4. a) A city with over 10 million people. [1]
   b) LICs. [1]
5. People/society; [1] environment; [1] economy. [1]
6. Solar panels [1] and well insulated homes [1] means less energy [1] from burning fossil fuels is used. [1]

Pages 98–101 Practice Questions

Page 98: Development
1. a) Development measures how advanced a country is. [1]
   b) Social; economic; environmental. (Any two indicators for [2].)
   c) Life expectancy; infant mortality; literacy rates; birth rate; access to clean water. (Any three examples for [3].)
   d) Gross Domestic Product (GDP); GDP per capita; type of industry. (Any two for [2].)
2. Primary industries dominate in LICs; [1] for example fishing, [1] farming, [1] mining. [1]
3. Severe climatic conditions such as drought [1] leave soils infertile and unproductive, [1] for example in the Sahel. Natural hazards such as floods or earthquakes [1] mean money must be spent on recovering from these disasters, [1] for example in Bangladesh.
4. The Brandt Line is misleading and outdated [1] because many countries below the line are in fact NICs (India and China). [1]
5. Because it shows the connection between economic and social development; [1] (plus [3] for considering why this is useful, for example, helps us to consider the human and physical factors that may affect development; allows us to assist development in a more appropriate way).
6. Attached [1]; donor [1]; recipient [1]; environment [1]; Corrupt [1]; dependency [1].
7. a) Sustainable development aims to help present and future generations. [1] If this to be successful then money must form just one part of the development process. [1] Economic sustainability, [1] social sustainability [1] and environmental sustainability [1] must all be considered.
   b) Fair trade contributes to sustainable development by assisting social, environmental and economic progress. (Five marks for reference to how farmer; local community; environment; and local economy are assisted.) [5]

Page 99: Economic Activity
1. Companies carry out economic activities to make a profit. [1]
2. Teacher = tertiary (service); [1] coal miner = primary; [1] baker = secondary. [1]
3. a) Primary workers obtain natural resources from the ground or the sea, such as fish, coal, iron, wood. [2]
   b) Nurse, teacher, lawyer, shop assistant. (Any two for [2])
   c) A = 70%; [1] B = 28%; [1] C = 80%. [1]
4. a) Strawberries, asparagus, sweetcorn, green beans and apples. (Two answers for [2].)
   b) About 60%. [1]
5. Natural resources; [2] energy. [1]
6. a) India, Bangladesh or China. (Two answers for [2].)
   b) A 'sweatshop' factory is one that has poor working conditions [1] such as long hours or low wages. [1]
7. Office cleaner; [1] security guard. [1]

Page 100: Natural Resources
1. Natural resources are found in nature. [1]
2. Using resources sustainably means using them carefully so they will last longer [1] and be available to future generations. [1]
3. They will eventually run out. [1]
4. It can be used as a fuel [1] or for building [1] or for making paper. [1] (Any two for [2])
5. a) 25–30 years. [1]
   b) Coniferous trees are quick growing [1] so it is easy to plant new trees to replace those that are cut down. [1]
6. a) Mahogany or teak. [1]
   b) Preserving the rainforest prevents it being chopped down [1] and ensures rainforest wildlife do not lose their habitat. [1]
7. a) A fish farm is an artificial method [1] of growing fish for humans to eat. [1]
   b) On a factory ship fish are processed [1] and frozen [1] at sea.
8. a) Russia. [1]
   b) Natural gas is used in homes for heating [1] and cooking. [1]

Page 101: Ordnance Survey Maps
1. a) 7559 [2]
   b) i) 7857, [2] ii) 8261, [2] iii) 8454. [2]
   c) i) St Newlyn East, [2] ii) Bolingey, [2] iii) Goonhavern. [2]
   d) 3 km [2]

Pages 103–109 Revise Questions

Page 103 Quick Test
1. Geographic Information System.   2.   The police use a GIS for plotting crime data on a digital map.   3.   A line on a digital map might show a road or river.   4.   Digital maps in the UK are produced by the Ordnance Survey.

Page 105 Quick Test
1. Geographical Technology.   2.   Google Earth.   3.   In the Layers Panel you can switch different layers of information on or off.   4.   A satellite is an orbiting spacecraft that carries cameras and other equipment.

Page 107 Quick Test
1. Learning Outside the Classroom.   2.   Co-operation is important because fieldwork involves group work.   3.   A grid reference is an example of co-ordinates used on a map.   4.   A wind vane is used to record wind direction.

Page 109 Quick Test
1. Ordnance Survey.   2.   A fieldwork sketch is a drawing done outside during fieldwork.   3.   75% use public transport (the bus).   4.   A picture graph.

Pages 110–111 Practice Questions

Page 110: Geographic Information Systems
1. Hardware, [1] software [1] and digital data. [1]
2. A GIS can be used to view data on maps. [1]
3. a) Plotting crime data on a GIS provides a visual record that shows patterns of crime [1] and allows the police to target specific areas. [1]
   b) One from: ambulance service, water, gas and electricity suppliers, supermarkets. [1]
4. To see if the information links to the layer below. [1]
5. a) Things that occur at a particular point are shown as symbols, e.g. the altitude of a mountain. [1]
   b) Information such as roads, rivers and railway lines are shown as lines on a GIS layer. [1]
6. A ✓ D ✓ [2]
7. Information such as leisure facilities, waste disposal facilities, parks and open spaces, local footpaths and shopping centres. (Any two for [2].)
8. a) Google Earth is a virtual globe [1] with maps and other data shown as layers. [1]
   b) By using the zoom tool [1] to move from viewing on the global scale, [1] through the national scale [1] to the local scale. [1]

9. a) On a satellite image you can see settlements, roads and land use. (Two answers for [2].)
   b) Aerial photos. [1]

Page 111: Fieldwork

1. a) Learning Outside the Classroom (LOtC). [1]
   b) Outdoors = Taking photos; Conducting Surveys [2]. In the classroom = Displaying data; Analysing data; Drawing conclusions [3].
   c) Fieldwork can involve bad weather [1] and working in difficult environments, e.g. slippery rocks [1].
2. The results will be incorrect [1] and you could come to the wrong conclusion. [1]
3. Two from: types of shops; number of pedestrians; size of shop frontage. (Two answers for [2].)
4. To measure the speed [1] of a stream or river. [1]
5. Closed question. [1]
6. You might use a historical map when presenting your fieldwork data to show how something has changed [1] over time. [1]
7. a) If you were showing different amounts of something [1] in different categories; [1] then you would use a bar chart.
   b) A pictogram is a visual way of presenting data. [1]

Pages 112–117 Review Questions

Page 112: Development

1. a) Low Income Countries [1]
   b) e.g. Ethiopia. (Appropriate example for [1].)
2. Levels of health [1] and education. [1]
3. The average [1] age a person will live/reach. [1]
4. Possible answers: manufacturing, processing, construction. [1]
5. Newly Industrialised Country. [1]
6. Because the value of their exports is less than that of their imports, [1] and they spend much of their GDP repaying loans [1] borrowed from HICs. [1]
7. Child health; Reduced child mortality; An end to poverty; Universal education [4].
8. Sustainable development is development that meets the needs of the present [1] without compromising the ability of future generations [1] to meet their own needs. [1]

Page 113: Economic Activity

1. Primary, [1] secondary, [1] tertiary. [1]
2. Manufacture means to make something in a factory. [1]
3. a) Take it to market [1] to sell and earn money. [1]
   b) It usually ends up in HICs [1] such as the UK or USA. [1]
4. a) Farmers use chemicals to make crops grow [1], to kill pests [1] or to stop the spread of disease. [1] (Any two for [2])
   b) An arable farm grows crops [1] and a pastoral farm rears animals. [1]
5. Machines. [1]
6. a) In the UK we make cars, clothes, chemicals and food products. ([2] for two examples.)
   b) A TV [1] A smart phone [1].
7. Samsung. [1]

Page 114: Natural Resources

1. They can last indefinitely [1] if they are used in a sustainable way. [1]
2. We use it again. [1] Glass bottles or metal cans can be recycled. [1]
3. a) Softwood trees. [1]
   b) Over 100 years. [1]
   c) So that local people can have jobs [1] and so wood can be exported so that the government earns money. [1]
4. a) Humans collect fish, shellfish, prawns, seaweed, coral and salt from the sea. (Two correct items for [2].)
   b) Overfishing results in fish stocks declining [1] as there are not enough fish left to breed. [1]
5. a) 33% [1]
   b) It causes pollution, [1] including greenhouse gases that cause global warming. [1]
6. a) Oil is not an important fuel in our power stations. [1]
   b) Fertilisers [1] pesticides. [1]

Page 115: Ordnance Survey Maps

1. a) Six-figure grid references give the location of a square that is 100 m x 100 m [2]; a four-figure grid reference gives the location of a square 1 km x 1 km. [2]
   b) i) 802553 or 802554 [2], ii) 788538 [2]
   c) i) Church (with a steeple); [2] ii) caravan/camp site; [2] iii) tourist information. [2]
   d) i) 833559 [2], ii) 838554 [2], iii) 832552 [2]

Page 116: Geographic Information Systems

1. It helps to decide which vehicle to send to answer an emergency call. [1]
2. a) A GIS layer shows a set of information. [1] It could be land use, settlement, roads or relief. [1]
   b) You might switch a layer off if it wasn't relevant to your work [1] or you could switch a layer on if you wanted to analyse some new information. [1]
   c) A map. [1]
   d) Photo or satellite image. [1]
3. Areas such as lakes or forests or towns. [1]
4. Text is needed on a GIS layer to add names to the locations and features on a map. [1]
5. Allow you to fly automatically from one part of the world to another. [1] You can also fly under the sea and view the ocean floor. [1]

Page 117: Fieldwork

1. a) In the school grounds [1] In the local neighbourhood. [1]
   b) Data collection is the part of the fieldwork process carried out in the field. [1]
2. It is important because there are many things that could go wrong or be dangerous if people were not safety conscious. [1]
3. A georeferenced photo is one that has the co-ordinates recorded [1] so that you know where it was taken. [1]
4. Examples: width of beach; pebble size; types of waves. (Two answers for [2].)
5. a) An anonymous questionnaire is one where the name of the person answering the questions is not recorded. [1]
   b) An example might be: Which is your favourite take-away food? or a similar question with no choice of answers given. [2]
6. A choropleth map.
7. a)

| 60% | 23% | 12% | 5% | [4] |

   b)

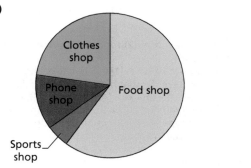

[4]

Pages 118–130 Mixed Test-Style Questions

1. a) Individuals carry out economic activities or work in order to earn money [1]. Companies carry out economic activities or business in order to make a profit. [1]
   b) People are involved in getting natural resources [1] from the ground [1] or from the sea. [1]
   c) i) True ii) False iii) False [3]
2. a) India, b) China, c) Russia [3]
3. a) i) Low GDP per capita South Korea $872, Kenya $1800. [1]
      ii) Lack of education; Kenya today = 87.4% adult literacy. [1]
      iii) High proportion of people working in agriculture; Kenya today = 75%. [1]

b) Rich country, $33 200 GDP per capita; [1] 12th largest economy in the world; [1] employment in high-tech industry, companies like Samsung and LG; [1] high quality education; [1] it is a democracy. [1] (Any three for [3])

4. a) i–iii) Corrasion (abrasion); [1] attrition; [1] hydraulic action; [1] solution. [1] (Any three for [3])
   b) i) Middle ii) Upper iii) Lower [3]

5. Non-renewable resources such as coal [1] are those natural resources which have taken millions of years to form and which will eventually run out. [1] Renewable resources such as copper [1] are those that can be recycled so that they can be used again [1] or some natural resources such as trees can be grown to replace those cut down. [1]

6. One argument for cutting down the trees in a rainforest is that it provides jobs for local people. [1] They need money to buy food and other goods. [1] One argument for not chopping down the trees in the rainforest is that the trees provide a natural habitat for wild animals [1] and without it, those wild animals will die. [1]

7. a) i) Nile; ii) Euphrates; iii) Tigris. (Any order) [3]
   b) Water supply; [1] useful for transport; [1] and/or trade; [1] fertile land due to silt left from flood water'. [1] (Any two for [2])
   c) Oil; [1] not every country has oil reserves. [1]

8. a) Granite = C, sandstone = A, Chalk = B. [3]
   b) Igneous rocks are hard/resistant to weathering/erosion, [1] contain mineral crystals, [1] are non-porous. [1]

9. The process [1] by which the proportion of people living in towns and cities grows. [1] (Must have word 'process' for [2].)

10. Using social [1] and economic [1] indicators such as GDP or life expectancy. [1]

11.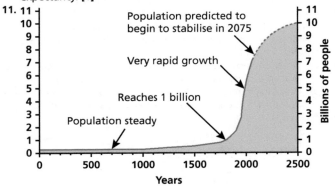

([2] for correctly labelled axes; [2] for correct graph; [2] for any two of annotations) [6]

12. The climate is usually not suitable, [1] e.g. it may be too cold [1] or there may be few resources [1] that humans need, e.g. food. [1]

13. a) Cold deserts: Gobi, Taklamakan (Any one for [1]); Hot deserts: Thar, Arabian, Rub'al Khali, Sahara. (Any one for [1])
    b) Similarities: Both types have low rainfall (precipitation) [1] Gobi = 194 mm a year, Arabian and Rub'al Khali = 30 mm a year. [1] Differences: cold deserts have low temperatures during the day time, Gobi = –40°C [1]; whereas hot deserts have very high day time temperatures: Thar desert = over 50°C . [1]

14. Tropical rainforests; [1]; savannah grasslands. [1]

15. a) If two plates move towards each other, this is called a destructive plate boundary. [1] At this boundary the rocks in the Earth's crust are heated and squeezed by great pressure [1] and pushed upwards to form mountains. [1]
    b) Conservative plate boundary [1]

16. a) Biological weathering. [1]
    b) Happens in cold, mountainous areas = Freeze-thaw weathering [1]
       Often occurs in deserts due to temperature change = Onion-skin weathering [1]
       Takes place when weak acid in rainwater dissolves rocks = Chemical weathering [1]
       Occurs when plants and animals break down rocks = Biological weathering [1]

17. a) Processes of weathering and erosion will carve out the glaciated landscape. [1] (Give explanation of at least two forms of weathering/erosion for extra [3] – freeze-thaw, plucking, abrasion.)
    b) Drumlin; moraine (Any one for [1])

18. People and jobs increase away from the city centre. [1] Urban centres no longer used for shopping and business; [1] so derelict factories, abandoned shops, poor quality housing, unemployment, crime, poor environment remains; [1] this is not an attractive place for people to live/work/shop. [1] (Any three for [3])

19. Rain is small droplets of liquid water. [1] Hail is pellets of solid ice. [1] Snow is made of tiny ice crystals arranged in patterns to form a snowflake. [1] Sleet is partly melted snow so is a mixture of ice and water. [1]

20. Wind speed [1] using an anemometer [1] and wind direction [1] using a wind vane. [1]

21. a) Ploughed field. [1]
    b) Trees and plants act as umbrellas and intercept rainfall before it hits the ground. [1] Tree and plant roots hold the soil together so that it is harder to wash away. [1] Trees act as windbreaks and reduce the effect of wind erosion on the soil. [1] Trees and plants store water from the ground, which reduces the amount of water available to flow over the soil surface. [1]
    c) Contour ploughing, [1] Building terraced fields, [1] Planting trees. [1]

22. Examples: i) Through tourism – 200 000 UK tourists visited Kenya in 2012. [1] ii) Through tea – Brook Bond owns and runs tea plantations in Kenya, and the tea is sold in UK shops. [1] iii) Through flowers – Kenyan flowers are sold in most UK supermarkets. [1]

23. a) They tell us about evolution. [1] Each part of the Geological Timescale has a set of rocks that contain particular plants or animals that lived at a certain time in the past [1] and the fossils help us to identify the age of the rocks and where they belong in the timescale. [1]
    b) Fish [1] Dinosaurs [1] Birds [1] Humans. [1]

24. Global temperatures fall (everywhere becomes cooler). [1] This results in more precipitation falling as snow in both temperate and polar areas. [1] As the snow builds up it forms glaciers and ice sheets that cover the land. [1] As less water returns to the oceans, sea levels fall. [1]

25. Rural to urban migration [1] means many people are moving to cities for work; [1] poorer countries are unable to provide home for these immigrants [1] who are forced to live in makeshift housing [1] close to the city. Due to the high rate of rural to urban migration in LICs shanty towns grow larger. [1]

26. a) Fieldwork is a process that involves several different stages. [1] Collecting data when out on fieldwork is an important first stage. [1] This data can then be used as evidence to answer fieldwork questions. The data can be presented as graphs or added to maps. [1] These can then be analysed so that fieldwork questions can be answered. [1]
    b) Examples: the type of shop or service using a simple classification; the number of different floors in each building; the condition of the building; the size of the shop front; the number of people entering the business per hour. ([1] per example to a maximum of [4])

27. The temperature [1] using a thermometer [1] and the wind speed [1] using an anemometer. [1] We might also record areas of shade and sunshine [1] on a map. [1] (Any four for [4])

28. a) Building dams; Creating reservoirs [2]
    b) One example of advantage and disadvantage of soft engineering and one example of advantage and disadvantage of hard engineering for [4]
       Examples: Advantages of hard engineering: groynes stop longshore drift carrying beach material away; [1] sea walls effectively reflect wave energy from eroding coast. [1] Disadvantages: expensive to maintain; [1] can look unattractive. [1] Advantages of soft engineering: beach nourishment is a more natural-looking method of coastal defence; [1] cheaper and more sustainable in the long term. [1]

Disadvantages: can be less effective; [1] managed retreat means valuable land may be lost. [1]

29. a) A GIS has many practical uses that can help people in real life. [1] It can make their job easier or safer or more effective. [1] The sorts of people that use GIS include transport companies, the police and other emergency services. [1] The police might use it to plot details of crimes that have taken place in particular locations. [1]

   b) You can have as many layers as you like in a GIS as it is possible to switch them off [1] if you don't want to see them or switch them on [1] when you want to use the information.

   c) A line is a linear feature [1] such as a river or road or railway [1] whereas a point is a feature found at a single location [1] such as a mountain peak or a building. [1]

30. Concerns to include five key issues: honeypot site attracting too many tourists; [1] overuse of footpaths leading to soil erosion; [1] dogs scaring/worrying the animals; [1] tourists leaving gates open meaning livestock get loose; [1] noise and water pollution in the lakes. [1]

31. Because workers are paid less so this makes the clothes cheaper [1] or because they are able to produce goods on a large scale to keep prices down. [1]

32. Most volcanoes give warning signs before they erupt [1] which gives people time to evacuate the area and move to a safe place. [1] Earthquakes happen very suddenly and without warning. [1]

33. The tropical climate and the desert climate both have very high temperatures all year round [1] but the tropical climate has a high rainfall [1] whereas the desert climate has little or no rainfall throughout the year. [1]

Glossary

ablation   when glacial ice melts

abrasion   when stones carried in the water scrape the river bed and banks

accumulation   when a glacier increases in size due to increased snowfall and less melting

aerial photo   a photo taken from the air, usually from an aeroplane

ageing population   a population that has a large and growing number of old people

agroforestry   growing trees and crops together

air pressure   the pressure resulting from the weight of the Earth's atmosphere

alpine tundra   environmental region found in upland areas where the ground is frozen all year and trees do not grow

altitude   the height of the land above sea level

Arab   member of an ethnic group originating in the Arabian Peninsula

Arabic   language spoken by Arabs

arable   a farm that grows crops such as wheat or potatoes

arch   a rock formation created from erosion and weathering

b

bar chart   a graph that plots points and then draws bars to represent the height

bedrock   solid rock found below soil that cannot be dug out by hand

biological weathering   when rocks are broken down by plants and animals

bi-polar scale   a type of rating scale with a continuum between two opposite end points or opinions

birth rate   the number of babies born per 1000 people per year in a particular country or area

Brandt Line   an imaginary line dividing the wealthier countries (above) and poorer countries (below)

British Empire   the countries and regions of the world that were once colonies of Great Britain

brown earth   type of soil found in the UK which is 1–2 metres deep with a thick topsoil layer

c

carbon sink   a natural store for carbon, e.g. rainforests

cardinal points   the four points of a compass: north, south, east and west

carrying capacity   the maximum number of people that the land can support

catchment area   area of land from which the rainfall drains into a particular river

chaebol   large South Korean company that produces a range of goods and services

chemical weathering   breaking up of rocks over time by weak acid contained in rainwater

chernozem   dark-coloured, fertile soil found in steppe regions

climate   the pattern of average temperature and average rainfall across the year

climate graph   a graph that combines data for temperature and rainfall at a particular location

climate zone   areas of the world that have the same pattern of temperature and rainfall

cold desert   environmental region of very low rainfall and low average daily temperatures

colony   group of people or country that is under the control of or occupied by settlers from another country

Communist   someone who holds the political belief that everything should belong to and be run by the government in order to create a fair and equal society

compass   device for determining the location of magnetic north or a diagram on a map showing the direction of north, south, east and west

conservative boundary   a plate boundary where two plates are sliding past each other

constructive boundary   a plate boundary where two plates are moving away from each other and new crust is being created from material rising up from the mantle

contour line   line joining points of equal height on a map

core   the very hot centre of the Earth

counterurbanisation   the movement of people from urban areas to smaller towns and villages

crust   the relatively thin layer of rocks that forms the outermost layer of the Earth

crystalline   minerals found in rocks that have a regular geometric shape

d

data   information that is collected during fieldwork activities

death rate   the number of deaths per 1000 people per year in a particular country or area

debt   when money is owed

deciduous   trees that lose their leaves in the autumn

deforestation   cutting down and removing of trees from an area

democracy   a political system where citizens have the right to vote for the government of the country

dense population   an area that has a relatively large number of people living there

dependency   to rely on another country as a main source of income

deposition   the process of transported material being deposited

desert climate   a climate with high temperatures all year round and little or no rainfall

desertification   when land becomes useless and unproductive for farming

destructive boundary   a plate boundary where two plates meet and one is destroyed as it moves beneath the other

differential erosion   erosion that happens at different rates (caused by the differing hardness/resistance of the rock types)

discordant   describes bands of different rocks

donor   a country that gives aid

dormant   describes a volcano that has not erupted in living memory but may erupt again in the future

drumlin   a tear-shaped mountain formed by glacial deposition

e

earthquake   a violent shaking of the Earth's crust caused by plate movement

emigrants   people who move out of a country

enquiry-based learning   learning by asking questions and trying to find answers

epicentre   the point where the earthquake shock waves reach the surface of the Earth and cause maximum damage

equator   an imaginary line drawn around the Earth at 00 latitude separating the northern and southern hemispheres

erratic   a large rock or boulder deposited far from its place of origin after glacial melt

erosion   the removal of weathered material by the action of wind, water or ice

ethnic group   people of the same race or nationality who share a particular culture

evolution   changes in living things over millions of years as they adapt to their changing environment

extinct   a plant or living creature that has died out; a volcano that will not erupt again

extrusive   igneous rocks that are formed on the surface of the Earth

f

factory ship   a very large ship that accompanies fishing boats then processes, freezes and stores the fish

fair trade   ensures that trade is beneficial to the LIC and not controlled unfairly by the HICs they trade with

family planning   advice about contraception and managing the number of children born

fieldwork   teaching and learning outside the classroom, usually away from the school

firn   a dense and compacted body of snow

fish farm   a place where fish are artificially bred and grown for human use

floodplain   an area of flat land bordering a river

focus   the point where an earthquake starts, usually deep underground

fossil   the remains of a living creature or plant trapped in a sedimentary rock

fossil fuel   a fuel formed from plants (coal) or ocean micro-organisms (oil and natural gas) trapped in sedimentary rock

freeze-thaw weathering   breaking up of rocks by water freezing and expanding in cracks

g

Geological Timescale   a timescale that shows when rocks and fossils were formed

Geographic Information System   a system consisting of hardware, software and data that allows geographical information to be plotted on maps and then studied

georeference   coordinates for a location so that it can be plotted on a map

geotechnology   technology that uses georeferenced data to create maps

glacial period   a period of cooling within an ice age

glaciation   a major cooling of the Earth leading to the formation of ice sheets that cover large areas

global warming   climate change in which the average temperature across the world increases

greenhouse gases   gases that trap heat, preventing it from escaping back into space

grid lines   lines drawn on OS maps running north to south and east to west

grid reference   a four- or six-figure number used to locate places on a map

Gross Domestic Product (GDP) per capita   total value of goods and services produced by a country in a year per head of population

h

hard engineering   the use of artificial materials to change the natural flow of the river

high income country (HIC)   a country with a gross national income per capita of US$12,616 or more

high-tech   using computers and other modern technology to make products such as phones, cameras and medical equipment

historical map   an old map that shows what the geography looked like in the past

honeypot   a tourist site that attracts large numbers of visitors

horizons   the layers found in soil

hot desert   environmental region with very low rainfall and high average daily temperatures

Human Development Index   a composite indicator for development; measures life expectancy, knowledge and standard of living

humid sub-tropical   environmental region found just north of the Tropic of Cancer and just south of the Tropic of Capricorn where the air is warm and holds a high percentage of moisture

humidity   the amount of moisture (water) in the air

humus   organic matter found in soil formed from decayed plants and animals

i

ice age   a time of extreme cooling of the Earth's climate where sheets of ice cover large areas of land

igneous   rocks formed from molten rock (magma)

immigrants   people who move into a country

independence   the act of a country separating from a colonial power and becoming self governing

indicators   used to measure and compare levels of development

indigenous   people who have historical ties to a particular area

interglacial period   a period of warmer climate within an ice age

intrusive   igneous rocks that are formed beneath the surface of the Earth

Islam   religion founded by the prophet Mohammed whose teachings are written in the Koran

l

labour   workers in a factory or other type of business

latosol   type of soil found in tropical regions which is 20–30 metres deep with a very thin topsoil layer

layer of information   a single set of information within a GIS

leaching   washing of minerals and nutrients through soil by water

Learning Outside the Classroom (LOtC)   any kind of learning that happens outside the classroom

levee   a natural deposit of sand and mud alongside a river

line   a series of locations that can be joined together to form a linear feature

line graph   a graph that plots points and then joins them up to form a line

lithified   the process of sediments becoming sedimentary rocks

longshore drift   the process of beach material being moved laterally due to the waves meeting the shore at a certain angle

low income country (LIC)   developing countries including much of Africa

m

mantle   the hot, semi-molten layer of rock that surrounds the Earth's core

manufacturing   making a product in a factory or workshop

maximum temperature   the highest recorded temperature in a day, month or year

meander   a curve or bend in the river

mechanised   the use of machinery to do work in factories or on farms

Mediterranean climate   climate characterised by hot, dry summers and warm, wet winters

megacity   a city with a population of 10 million or more

metamorphic   rocks that have been formed from igneous or sedimentary rocks subjected to heat and pressure

migration   the movement of people from one area or country to another area or country

mineral   a natural resource found in rock that is not made from plant or animal matter, e.g. gold, silver, diamonds, quartz, salt

minimum temperature   the lowest recorded temperature in a day, month or year

monsoon   climate characterised by a definite wet season and dry season

montane forest   tropical rainforest found in upland areas where there is very high humidity

moraine   the material deposited after the glacier has melted

Muslim   a follower of Islam

n

natural resources   products that humans use which have come from the land or the sea

Newly Industrialising Countries (NICs)   countries such as China and Brazil that have developed industries, often making products for HICs; countries experiencing rapid economic growth

nomadic pastoralists   traditional farmers who herd livestock from one place to another in search of water and grass

non-porous   rocks that do not hold water

non-renewable   a natural resource that cannot be replaced and will eventually run out

o

ocean current   a warm or cold flow of ocean water that moves long distances and affects climate

one-child policy   introduced in China as a a means of controlling population growth in 1979, it limited every family to having one child only

onion-skin weathering   splitting and flaking of a rock surface due to repeated heating and cooling

Ordnance Survey   the organisation that produces the maps that are most widely used in the UK

overfishing   catching too many fish so that there are not enough to breed naturally

p

parent material   the type of rock that the soil has been weathered from

pastoral   a farm where animals such as cattle or sheep are reared

perception   what we think about something (our opinion)

permafrost   ground found in tundra regions where the subsoil is frozen all year round

pictogram   a symbol used on a graph

plate   a section of the Earth's crust

plate boundary   the line along which two plates meet

plucking   when rocks become frozen to and removed by the glacier

point   a particular location on a digital map

polar climate   a climate with low rainfall and low temperatures throughout the year

polygon   a series of locations that can be joined together to enclose an area of any shape

population density   a statistic showing the number of people living in a square kilometre of land

population distribution   the way in which people are spread across the world or a particular area

population growth   the increase in the number of people in a particular country or area

porous   rocks that are able to hold water

poverty   a lack of money to buy the essential things that people need to live

power station   a place where electricity is generated by using fuel to heat water and power turbines

precipitation   different types of water that fall from clouds (rain, hail, sleet and snow)

primary activity   a job that involves obtaining natural resources from the land or sea

q

quality of life   a statistic that measures people's ability to buy or find enough resources to meet their daily needs

r

raw data   data that hasn't been processed or altered in any way

reaforrestation   when trees are planted in deforested areas

recipient   a country receiving an aid donation

recycle   use resources again and again to extend their life

refugees   people who flee from their own country due to war or natural disasters

relief   the shape of the land

renewable   a natural resource that can be replaced so it is always around

retail   shops selling goods and services

retreat   warmer temperatures will cause glaciers to melt and decrease in size

Richter scale   a measure of the energy released (magnitude or size) by an earthquake

rural to urban migration   the process of people moving from the countryside into cities

s

satellite imagery   photos of the Earth taken from space taken by a satellite

savannah grasslands   environmental region of grassland with few trees found in tropical and sub-tropical countries

scale lines   lines drawn on the edge of a map to indicate how far a distance on the map is in reality

sea level   the point where the land meets the sea

secondary activity   a job that involves making a product, often in a factory

sedimentary   rocks formed from deposits that are originally from older rocks and living organisms

self-help scheme   a scheme giving local people ownership of land and tools, and offering help to improve their own living conditions

semi-arid   environmental region with little rainfall, usually 200–500 mm a year

service   an activity that helps people or organisations in some way

shanty town   an area of makeshift housing built on unwanted land on the outskirts of a city

snout   the end of the glacier

soft engineering   the use of natural measures to reduce flood risk

soil erosion   the removal of soil from the landscape by the action of wind and water

sparse population   an area that has relatively few people living there

spot height   point on a map indicating the height above sea level

stack   a rock formation caused by erosion; formed when an arch collapses

steppe   environmental region found in northern Europe and Asia consisting of grassland and few trees

stump   a rock formation caused by erosion; formed when an arch collapses to leave a stack and the stack decreases

subsoil   soil that is found below topsoil

sub-tropical   environmental region located just north of the Tropic of Cancer or just south of the Tropic of Capricorn

suburbanisation   the growth and development of residential areas just outside towns and cities

sustainable   careful use of resources so that we have enough for now and for future generations

sustainable city   a city that offers a good quality of life for residents, without compromising the quality of life for future residents

sustainable development   development that meets the needs of present generations without compromising the ability of future generations to meet their own needs

t

taiga (boreal forest)   environmental region of evergreen, coniferous forests

tectonic plate   a section of the Earth's crust

temperate climate   a climate that has high rainfall all year with mild winters and cool summers

temperature range   the difference between the maximum and minimum temperatures

terracing   building fields up in steps on a slope to enable farming to take place and to minimise erosion

tertiary activity   a job that involves providing a service to individuals or companies

textiles   cloth made from natural or artificial fibres and usually used to make clothes

topsoil   the layer of soil on the surface of the ground

trade deficit   more money is spent on buying goods (imports) than is made on selling goods (exports)

transportation   the process of eroded material being carried along

triangulation point   a reference point used by cartographers to draw maps accurately

tropical climate   a climate that has high temperatures and high rainfall all year

tropical equatorial forest   another name for tropical rainforest

tropical rainforest   ecosystem consisting of a very high density of forest vegetation and wildlife found between latitude 28°N and 28°S

tropical typhoon   large-scale low pressure system that develops in warm seas in the Indian and Pacific Oceans, characterised by strong winds, and heavy rainfall

tropical wet   environmental region either side of the Equator between latitude 23°N and 23°S with high levels of rainfall over 2500 mm

tsunami   a large wave caused by an undersea earthquake

tundra   environmental region where it is so cold that trees do not grow and the ground is frozen all year round

u

urban decline   the decline of an urban area, characterised by unemployment, crime, poverty and poor quality housing

urbanisation   the increase in the population in urban areas

urban regeneration   the revival of a run-down urban area through investment

v

virtual globe   a computer-generated image of the Earth

volcano   a mountain formed when molten magma escapes from the mantle and flows as lava on the Earth's surface

w

waterfall   a vertical drop where water flows over; part of a river or stream

wave-cut notch   an indentation in the base of a cliff, where the waves have eroded it

wave-cut platform   a sloping rock ledge at the base of cliffs, created by erosion

weather   daily changes in the atmosphere that affect humans

weathering   breakdown of rocks by the action of weather, water, chemicals and living things

working age   the group of people in a population aged roughly 16–65 years

Index

Collins

KS3 Geography

Workbook

David Rayner and Alison Farrell

Contents

KS3 Geography Workbook

Contents

Place Knowledge

Location Knowledge – Russia

1 **a)** **i)–v)** Fill in the labels on the map to show five of the countries that share a land border
with Russia. [5]

   b) **vi)–ix)** Label the following cities on the map:

   Moscow   **St Petersburg**   **Omsk**   **Vladivostok** [4]

   c) Russia's longest river is shown on the map. What is the name of this river? [1]

   ....

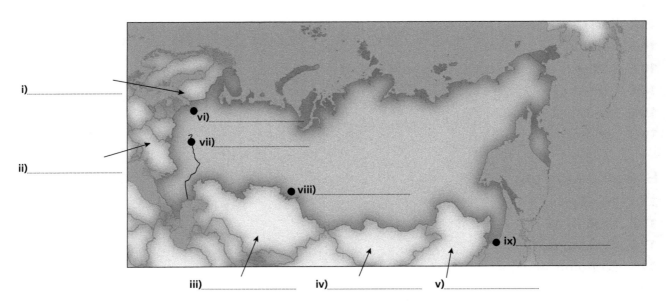

2 Give a brief description of each of the following environmental regions in Russia.

   a) Steppe: ....

   ....

   .... [2]

   b) Taiga: ....

   ....

   .... [2]

   c) Tundra: ....

   ....

   .... [2]

   Total Marks .... / 16

Location Knowledge – China

1 **a) i)–vi)** Fill in the labels on the map to show six of the countries that share a land border with China. [6]

b) vii)–x) Label the following cities on the map:

vii   ix   x   viii
| **Beijing**   **Chongqing**   **Shanghai**   **Tianjin** [4]
                       3   4   2

c) Name the two rivers labelled A and B on the map.

A _Yellow R_   **B** _Yangtze R_ [2]

ii 2 Nepal
III 3 Myanmar
IV 4 Vietnam
✓ 5 N korea
vi 1 Mongolia

i)

2 ii)

vi)

v)

vii)

viii)

A

B

ix) Chong

x)

3 iii)

iv) 4

2 **a)** Describe the One Child Policy in China.

[2]

b) Describe the population features of China's cities.

[3]

Total Marks .... / 17

Place Knowledge

Location Knowledge – India

1 **a) i)–v)** Fill in the labels on the map to show five of the countries that share a land border with India. [5]

b) One of India's major rivers is shown on the map. What is the name of this river?

_____ [1]

c) vi)–ix) Label the following cities on the map: [4]

Delhi *vi* ①   Chennai *ix* ④   Bangalore *viii* ③   Mumbai *vii* ②

1 Paki
2 Bang.
3 Myanmar
4 Nep
5 China

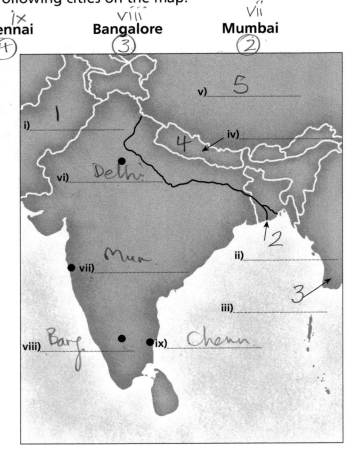

v) ___5___
i) ___1___
iv) ___4___
vi) ___Delhi___
ii) ___2___
iii) ___3___
vii) ___Mum___
viii) ___Barg___
ix) ___Chenn___

2 Give a brief description of India's economy.

_____

_____

_____

_____

_____ [2]

Total Marks _____ / 12

Location Knowledge – The Middle East

1 **a)** **i)–ix)** Fill in the labels on the map to show nine of the countries in the Middle East region. [9]

b) Name the other eight countries that make up the Middle East region.

....

....

.... [8]

c) **x)–xii)** Label the following cities on the map:

Cairo   **Tehran**   **Baghdad**   [3]

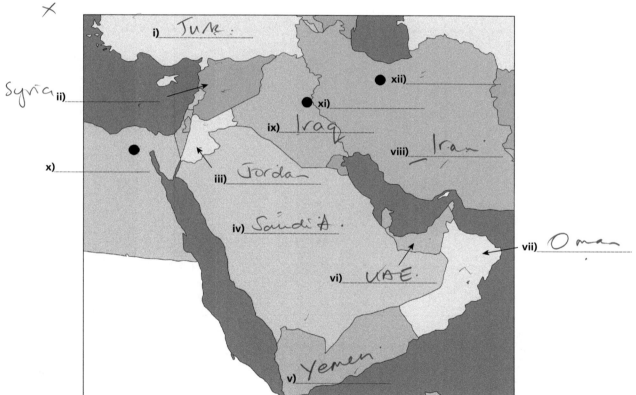

i) Turk.

Syria ii)

x)

iii) Jordan

ix) Iraq

xi)

xii)

viii) Iran

iv) Saudi A.

vi) UAE.

vii) Oman

v) Yemen.

2 Name the three longest rivers in the Middle East.

....

.... [3]

3 How do the richest countries in the Middle East gain their wealth?

.... [1]

Total Marks .... / 24

Place Knowledge

Africa and Asia Compared – Kenya

1 **a) i)–v)** Fill in the labels on the map to show the countries that share a land border with Kenya. [5]

b) vi)–vii) Fill in the labels on the map to show the two lakes that form part of Kenya's border. [2]

c) viii)–ix) Label the following cities on the map:

Nairobi   **Mombasa** [2]

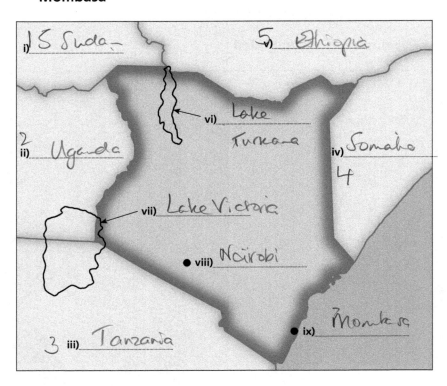

i) S Sudan
ii) Uganda 2
iii) Tanzania 3
iv) Somalia 4
v) Ethiopia 5
vi) Lake Turkana
vii) Lake Victoria
viii) Nairobi
ix) Mombasa

2 Give a brief description of Kenya's Great Rift Valley.

_____
_____
_____ [3]

3 Describe the current population in Kenya.

_____
_____
_____ [4]

Total Marks _____ / 16

Africa and Asia Compared – South Korea

1 **a) i)–iii)** Fill in the labels on the map to show the countries that are close neighbours with South Korea. [3]

b) iv)–vii) Label the following cities on the map:

Seoul   **Busan**   **Incheon**   **Daegu**   [4]

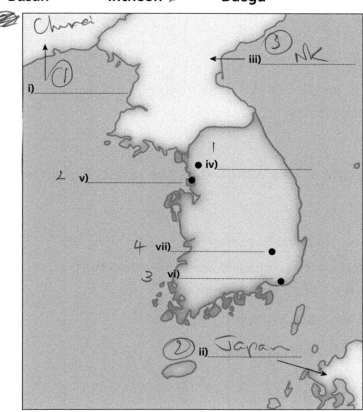

2 Name the two main rivers in South Korea.

.... [2]

3 Name four of South Korea's chaebols.

....

.... [4]

4 What did the 2011 EU Free Trade Agreement mean for South Korea?

....

.... [2]

Total Marks .... / 15

Physical Geography

Geological Timescale

1 The diagram shows the remains of ancient creatures trapped in layers of rock.

a) What kind of rock have the creatures been trapped in?

Igneous rock ☐

Sedimentary rock ☐

Metamorphic rock ☐ [1]

b) What name is given to the remains of living things preserved in the rock layers?

.... [1]

c) Which numbered layer of rock is likely to be the oldest? Explain why.

....

.... [2]

2 The diagram shows part of the Geological Timescale called the Mesozoic Era, and is divided into three periods.

a) How long did the Mesozoic Era last?

.... million years. [1]

65		Cretaceous
144	MESOZOIC	
206		Jurassic
248		Triassic

b) Which period of the Mesozoic was the longest? .... [1]

c) What type of rock now commonly found in the UK was formed during this period?

.... [1]

d) How do we know that the UK was submerged beneath a warm tropical sea during this time?

.... [1]

e) What type of creatures were very common during the Mesozoic Era?

.... [1]

f) What happened to these creatures at the end of the Mesozoic Era?

.... [1]

3 Match the dates below to the statements by drawing lines between the boxes. [4]

4.6 billion years ago	The time when humans appeared on Earth.
350 million years ago	The time when the Earth was first formed.
2.3 million years ago	The time when reptiles and flying insects first appeared.
3.5 billion years ago	The time when the first life appeared on Earth in the oceans.

4 Humans are primates and descended from apes. Humans belong to a group of apes called 'hominids'. Our closest living relative is the chimpanzee.

a) On which continent is it believed that the first humans appeared?

.... [1]

b) What name is given to the process of change that happened in the diagram above?

.... [1]

c) Describe the two main changes shown in the diagram above.

....

.... [2]

d) How did the first humans get food?

.... [2]

e) What are the two skills that humans developed that made them very different from their ancestors?

.... [2]

Total Marks .... / 22

Physical Geography

Plate Tectonics

1 On the outline, draw a cross-section of the Earth to show the different layers. Label the layers and indicate the rough thickness of each layer in kilometres.

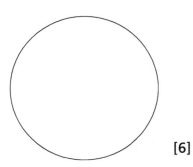

[6]

2 Match the words to the definitions by drawing lines between the boxes.　　　[4]

Crustal plates	A plate that is very thick with a mountain range lying on top.
Plate boundary	A plate that has very thin crust with an ocean lying on top.
Oceanic crust	The line along which two crustal plates meet.
Continental crust	The individual sections of the Earth's crust.

3 Study the diagram below.

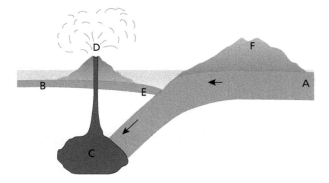

Insert the correct letters into the boxes.

	Earthquakes will occur here where the two plates rub together.
	A volcano has been formed where hot rock reaches the surface.
	A plate made of thick continental crust.
	The continental plate has been squeezed and pushed up to form mountains.
	The oceanic plate is melting and the hot rock is rising back up to the surface.
	A plate made of thin oceanic crust.

[6]

4 The North American Plate and the Pacific Plate are sliding past each other along the San Andreas Fault.

a) What type of plate boundary is this?

_____ [1]

b) Which of the following statements is correct? Tick the correct answer.

    i) Crust is being destroyed along the San Andreas Fault.

    ii) Crust is being created along the San Andreas Fault.

    iii) Crust is neither being created nor destroyed along the San Andreas Fault. [1]

c) What type of natural disaster is likely to happen in San Francisco?

_____ [1]

5 The diagram shows a cross-section of the Earth's crust. The circles represent the shockwaves from an earthquake which started at point A.

a) What names are given to points A and B?

Point A _____

Point B _____ [2]

b) Which house will be damaged most by the earthquake? Explain why.

_____

_____ [2]

c) Why might the houses be destroyed by fires during an earthquake?

_____

_____ [2]

d) If an earthquake happened under the sea, what kind of natural disaster might result?

_____ [1]

Total Marks _____ / 26

Physical Geography

Rocks and Geology

1 **a)** Draw two diagrams to show the difference between porous and non-porous rock.

| | |
| | |

[3]

b) Which of the following rocks are **porous** and which are **non-porous**?

   i)   Clay   ....

   ii)   Chalk   ....

   iii) Granite   ....

   iv) Sandstone   ....

   v)   Slate   ....

   vi) Basalt   ....   [6]

2 Which of the following is a **true** statement about *all* sedimentary rocks? Tick the correct option.

Sedimentary rocks are formed from the remains of dead organisms. ☐

Sedimentary rocks are formed from deposits of older rocks that have been worn down by erosion. ☐

Sedimentary rocks are porous, which makes them easier to erode and weather. ☐

Sedimentary rocks are formed from the remains of dead organisms and deposits from weathered and eroded older rocks. ☐ [2]

3 Circle the odd one out in each group and then give a reason for your choice.

a) **Sedimentary rocks**   **Metamorphic rocks**   **Igneous rocks**   [1]

Reason: ....

....

[2]

b) **Exfoliation**   **Freeze–thaw**   **Oxidation**   [1]

Reason: ....

....

[2]

c) **Marble**   **Sandstone**   **Slate**   [1]

Reason: ....

....

[2]

d) **Basalt**   **Carboniferous limestone** **Chalk**   [1]

Reason: ....

....

[2]

4 The photograph shows a fossil.

How were fossils formed?

....

....

[2]

Total Marks .... / 25

Physical Geography

Weathering and Soil

1 Match each type of weathering to its description.

Weathering type	Description
Chemical weathering	Layers of rock flake off due to expansion and contraction
Freeze–thaw weathering	Rocks are broken down by plants and animals
Onion-skin weathering	Weak acid dissolves rock
Biological weathering	Pieces of rock break off due to expansion

[4]

2 The following are four descriptions of types of weathering. The descriptions have been muddled up. Put the letters in the correct order to show the order in which weathering occurs. Then give the name of the type of weathering described.

a) A Limestone rots and crumbles away.

    B Limestone is made of calcium carbonate.

    C Calcium carbonate reacts with weak acid in rainwater.

    D Rain falls on an exposed area of limestone.

    Correct order: _____ [2]

    Type of weathering: _____ [1]

b) A In hot places the sun heats up rocks making them expand.

    B The outside surface of the rock begins to flake and break off.

    C The surface of the rock cools down more quickly than the middle.

    D At night temperatures drop very quickly.

    Correct order: _____ [2]

    Type of weathering: _____ [1]

c) A Eventually the roots cause the rocks to split apart.

    B Animals can then cause rocks to break further because of burrowing.

    C The plant grows and its roots widen the crack.

    D Plant seeds get into the cracks in rocks.

    Correct order: _____ [2]

    Type of weathering: _____ [1]

d) **A** Temperatures drop below freezing.

B Water gets into the cracks in rocks.

C The ice puts pressure on the rocks and they split apart.

D Water freezes in the cracks and expands.

Correct order: .... [2]

Type of weathering: .... [1]

3 **a)** Look at the list below. Put a tick or a cross beside each, depending on whether or not it is a component of soil.

Dead plants ☐   Water ☐

Dead animals ☐   Air ☐

Minerals ☐   Worms ☐   [6]

b) Now complete the pie chart using the following information.

Minerals – 45%   Water – 25%   Air – 25%   Organic matter – 5%

[4]

4 Match each soil horizon with its description.

Horizon	Description
B	Parent material: the rock type that the soil is formed from.
O	Sub soil where weathered rock is becoming part of the soil.
A	Surface layer consisting of surface layers and twigs.
R	Top soil rich in nutrients, minerals and humus.
C	Bedrock, solid rock that cannot be dug out by hand.

[5]

Total Marks .... / 31

Physical Geography

1 The data in the table below has been collected at a weather station. Add the following labels to the table to indicate which data belongs to which type of weather.

Rainfall   Wind speed   Wind direction   Air pressure   Temperature   Humidity

Weather data	90%	15 mm	6°C	North west	1012 mb	30 mph
Weather type						

[6]

2 Precipitation is the name given to all the types of water that fall from clouds. Underline the precipitation types that are solid and circle those that are liquid.

Hail   Rain   Snow [3]

3 Using the formula below, match each letter to the correct term.

$$A = B - C$$

Minimum temperature ☐

Temperature range ☐

Maximum temperature ☐ [3]

4 This weather map shows the weather forecast for Great Britain.

Describe the differences between the weather forecast for Wales and the weather forecast for Scotland.

_____

_____

_____

_____

_____

_____

_____

_____

[4]

5 Air pressure is a measure of the weight of the air. Put the correct words into the spaces in the sentence below.

increases   **low**   **decreases**   **high**

When air rises, the air pressure _____ and when air sinks, the air pressure _____.

Air moves from areas of _____ pressure to areas of _____ pressure.   [4]

6 Clouds and rain may form for many reasons. Number the following phrases 1–5 to put them in the correct order to demonstrate one of these reasons.

a) Warm air is lighter and rises.   ☐

b) The sun heats the ground.   ☐

c) As air rises it cools and clouds form.   ☐

d) The air near the ground becomes warm.   ☐

e) Clouds may produce rain or snow.   ☐   [5]

7 Plot the following data on an outline climate graph like the one below. The rainfall data should be plotted as a bar graph and the temperature data as a line graph.

Months	Jan	Feb	Mar	Apr	May	Jun	Jul	Aug	Sep	Oct	Nov	Dec
Rainfall (mm)	35	30	30	25	20	10	5	5	15	25	30	40
Temperature (°C)	5	7	9	10	14	18	21	24	22	16	12	8

[10]

Total Marks _____ / 35

Physical Geography

Glaciation

1 Number these statements 1–4 to put them in the right order to describe how glaciers are formed.

    a) The process is very slow and takes hundreds of years. ☐

    b) Over time, the weight of the accumulated snow causes it to become dense and compacted and it turns to ice. ☐

    c) When more snow falls than can melt, snow builds up. ☐

    d) The weight of the ice causes it to slide downhill. ☐   [4]

2 Below is a photograph of a glaciated valley in the Lake District. Label the following landforms: ribbon lake, truncated spur, U-shaped valley.

[3]

3 Number these statements 1–7 to put them in the right order to describe how corries are formed.

6 **a)** Rock frozen to the bottom of the ice erodes the base of the hollow making it deeper. ☐

3 **b)** The ice freezes to the bedrock at the back of the hollow. ☐

4 **c)** Under the weight of the ice, and the effects of gravity, the ice begins to slip. ☐

2 **d)** The snow compacts to form glacial ice. ☐

5 **e)** As the ice slips, it plucks rocks from the back of the hollow. ☐

7 **f)** After a very long time, the ice makes the hollow deep with a steep back wall. ☐

1 **g)** Snow builds up in a hollow at the top of a mountain. ☐   [7]

4 Glaciated landscapes are 'honeypot' sites. Explain to a friend in a tweet (140 characters) what you understand 'honeypot' site to mean.

[Blank grid table]

[2]

5 People use glaciated landscapes for different reasons. Not all of these reasons are compatible.

Complete the conflict matrix below by putting a tick if you think the groups will agree and a cross if you think they will disagree with how each other is using an area. If you are not sure, put a question mark.

Local residents	Hill walkers	Motor boaters	Conservationists	
				Farmers
				Local residents
				Hill walkers
				Motor boaters

[2]

6 Design a poster to help local residents explain their concerns about motor boaters' and hill walkers' use of their local environment (both the landscape and the towns).

[Blank box]

[5]

Total Marks .... / 23

Physical Geography

1 Describe the formation of a waterfall.

Use the diagram to help you.

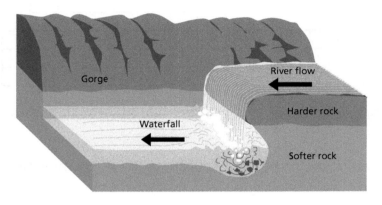

....

....

....

....

....

....

....

....   [6]

2 How is hydraulic action different at the coast than in rivers?

....

....

....

....   [2]

3 Explain why it is important to understand the difference between harder and softer rock when studying coastal and river landforms.

....

....

....

....   [3]

4 Describe how urbanisation contributes to flooding.

....

....

.... [3]

5 Explain how constructive waves build beaches.

....

....

....

.... [4]

6 Describe two benefits of hard engineering in coastal environments.

1 ....

....

....

2 ....

....

.... [4]

7 Managed retreat is a controversial approach to coastal erosion. Identify one group who will be **for** managed retreat and one group who would be **against** it. Explain each point of view.

For: ....

....

....

....

Against: ....

....

....

.... [6]

Total Marks .... / 28

Physical Geography

1 Use the images below to help identify four different ways humans benefit from their natural environment.

1 ....

2 ....

3 ....

4 .... [4]

2 Describe what makes an environment 'fragile'.

....

.... [2]

3 Annotate the cartoon below to explain why rainforests are referred to as 'carbon sinks'.

[5]

4 There are a number of strategies for sustainable management in rainforests.

Draw lines between the boxes to match up each strategy to how it works.

Strategy	How it works

Strategy	How it works
Reafforestation	Creating protected areas of rainforest
Conservation	Planting crops amongst the trees to prevent soil erosion
Agro-forestry	Monitor illegal deforestation and disruption to indigenous people
Satellite photography	Planting trees to replace the ones cut down

[4]

5 Identify three ways savannah grasslands can be classified as fragile environments.

....

....

.... [3]

6 Describe how each of the sustainable management strategies for savannah grasslands works.

Strategy	How it works
Reduce grazing	
'Magic stones'	
Planting trees	
Drought-resistant plants	
Terracing	

[5]

Human Geography

1 a) How do we write the world population of 7 250 000 000 people in words?

_____ [1]

b) What percentage (approximately) of the world's population lives in the two most populous countries? Circle the correct answer.

China = 1 300 000 000   India = 1 200 000 000

14%   34%   44%   64%   [1]

2 Although the world has experienced a 'population explosion' in the last 200 years, the number of babies being born is decreasing. This is likely to have a big impact on future world population as people are also living longer.

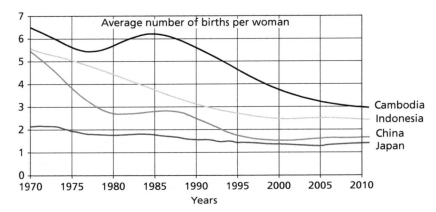

a) The number of births per woman was already low in Japan 40 years ago. What has happened to the average number of births since 1970?

_____ [1]

b) China and Indonesia both started off with similar numbers of births in 1970. Describe, using data, how the number of births has changed in the two countries since then.

_____

_____

_____

_____ [4]

c) In 1970, it was predicted the world population would grow to 12 billion people by 2050. Why has that prediction now been changed to 10 billion people?

_____

_____ [2]

3 Complete the table below by adding the words **dense** or **sparse** in the correct boxes.

Type of land	Population Density
Marshland	
Fertile land	
Land covered by ice	
Desert	
Flat land	

[5]

4 **a)** Rank the countries listed below from highest to lowest population density. [1]

Countries	South Korea	Egypt	UK	Russia	Peru
People per sq km.	495	85	260	10	25

b) Plot the data on the graph below. Put the countries in the order you gave in part **a)**.

People per km²

Countries

[5]

5 Describe a link between poverty and high death rates in Low Income Countries (LICs).

[2]

Total Marks .... / 22

Human Geography

1 Complete the table below by adding:

a) Reasons people are attracted to cities to live and work.	b) Reasons people leave their homes in the countryside to live in cities.	c) Reasons why the decision might be difficult for people to take.

[9]

2 Describe one problem with urbanisation and two sustainable solutions to the problem you have identified. Use the diagram below to help you.

Problem with urbanisation		Sustainable solution
		Sustainable solution

[3]

3 Look carefully at the photograph below of Rocina, the largest favela in Rio de Janeiro.

a) Complete the environmental quality survey for the favela.

	+3	+2	+1	−1	−2	−3	
Spacious							Crowded
Flat land							Steep land
Well planned							Unplanned
Quality building materials							Poor building materials
Well kept roads and pavements							No roads and pavements

[2]

b) What does the completed survey suggest about Rocina?

....

.... [3]

c) Why do you think people still live in places like this?

....

....

.... [3]

Total Marks .... / 20

Human Geography

Development

1 **a)** Classify the indicators below into social indicators or economic indicators by writing each one in the correct table.

Literacy rate   **GDP per capita**   **Infant mortality rate**

Gross Domestic Product   **Life expectancy**   **Primary industries**

Tertiary industries   **Secondary industries**   [8]

Social Indicator	Up or down

Economic Indicator	Up or down

b) Write down whether each indicator will go **up** or **down** as a country becomes more developed. [8]

2 Being reliant on the export of primary goods helps to explain why some countries are less developed than others.

Number the following statements 1–4 to put them in the correct order and show how each factor affects a country's ability to develop.

a) The country won't have as much money to invest in health and education. ☐

b) The country will find it difficult to build up secondary industries. ☐

c) The country won't earn much money for the materials they sell. ☐

d) Primary products are relatively low value. ☐ [4]

3 Put a tick next to the measures listed below that are included in the Human Development Index.

Doctors per person ☐

% agricultural land ☐

Life expectancy ☐

Number of years at school ☐

Access to electricity ☐

Gross national income (GNI) per capita ☐

Adult literacy ☐

[4]

4 Put the letter corresponding to each of these statements about fair trade into the appropriate places in the sustainable development Venn diagram below. [9]

A Environment is protected by traditional farming practices.

B The farmer is paid a fair price.

C Fair trade dividend goes to community groups.

D Community groups hold meetings to discuss their needs.

E People are elected to represent their communities.

F Farmers can grow crops in traditional ways which protect the environment.

G Communities choose what is best for them.

H Products have a stable price

I Communities can put in place long-term plans.

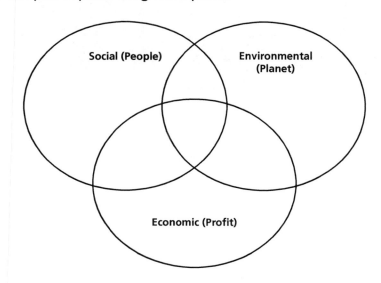

Total Marks _____ / 33

Human Geography

1 Economic activity is defined as human actions that deal with the production, distribution and consumption of goods and services. Draw lines to match the words to the definitions.

[3]

| Production | | is the selling and buying of goods in shops. |

| Distribution | | is the making of goods in factories and workshops. |

| Consumption | | is the transport of goods from factories to shops. |

2 Look at the people shown below. Classify their type of work by adding one of the following labels underneath each one:

Primary   Secondary   Tertiary   [4]

I work on a farm driving a tractor. We grow wheat.

I work in a factory making lawn mowers. I put the motor into each machine.

I work in a jewellery workshop making beautiful bracelets.

I work in an estate agents helping people buy and sell their homes.

....

3 Explain why factories need each of the following things:

a) Land ....

b) Natural resources ....

c) Energy ....

d) Labour ....

e) Transport ....[5]

4 Look at the data shown below and decide which country is an LIC and which country is an HIC.

Country A

Primary workers	Secondary workers	Tertiary workers
5%	18%	77%

Country B

Primary workers	Secondary workers	Tertiary workers
47%	12%	41%

Country A is a _____ and Country B is a _____. [2]

5 In the UK, some of the food we buy cannot be grown in this country. Other food can be grown in the UK but is imported simply because we want to eat it all year round.

Tick the fruit shown below that cannot be grown in the UK.

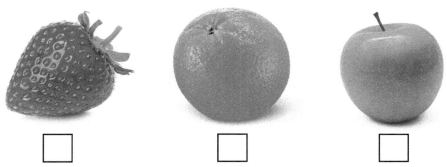

[1]

☐   ☐   ☐

6 Complete the sentences below by adding the correct words.

mechanised   organic   pastoral   arable

a) _____ farming uses lots of modern machinery to get the work done as efficiently as possible.

b) _____ farming involves rearing animals. These could be cattle, sheep, goats or llamas.

c) _____ farming involves growing crops. These could include fruit, vegetables and herbs.

d) _____ farming means using no chemicals on the farm. Only natural fertilisers and means of controlling pests are allowed. [4]

Total Marks _____ / 19

Human Geography

Natural Resources

1 Which of the following items are natural resources and which are man-made resources? Tick the correct column.

	Natural resource	Man-made resource
Coal		
Glass		
Marble		
Wood		
Plastic		
Water		

[6]

2 Study the graph below showing the amount of haddock caught by fishing boats in the North Sea.

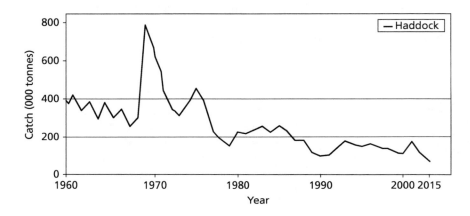

Next to each statement, write **true** or **false**:

a) The peak catch of haddock was in 1975. ....

b) The amount of haddock caught has roughly halved over the last 50 years. ....

c) There is no problem with overfishing in the North Sea. .... [3]

3 a) Why is it a good idea to plant two young trees every time one of the mature trees in a forest is cut down? Use the word 'sustainable' in your answer.

....

....

....

.... [2]

b) If you wanted to grow a new forest relatively quickly, what sort of trees would you plant and why?

....

....

.... [2]

4 Many natural resources will run out in the near future as they are non-renewable. It is a good idea to recycle as many waste products as possible.

a) What does non-renewable mean?

....

.... [1]

b) Which of the waste products listed below come from non-renewable resources and which one comes from a renewable resource?

Drink cans ....   Plastic bottles ....

Glass bottles ....   Paper .... [4]

c) Why is it a good idea to recycle waste products that are non-renewable?

....

.... [1]

d) Give one other good reason why it makes sense to recycle products of all kinds.

....

.... [1]

Total Marks .... / 20

Geography Skills

Ordnance Survey Maps

Look at the Ordnance Survey map and answer the following questions.

180   KS3 Geography Workbook

You have decided to walk part of the Beacons Way.

1 **a)** You park at **988198**. What facilities can you find there?

.... [1]

b) From here follow the Beacons Way to Corn Du. Which direction are
you walking?

.... [1]

c) How far do you have to walk to reach Corn Du?

.... [2]

d) How high have you climbed?

.... [2]

2 There are three other hills you want to walk to – Pen y Fan, Cribyn and Fan y Big.

Give the six-figure grid reference and spot height for each of them.

a) Pen y Fan .... [3]

b) Cribyn .... [3]

c) Fan y Big .... [3]

3 From Fan y Big you look south west and see a reservoir with a small island in it.

a) Give the four-figure grid reference for the reservoir.

.... [1]

b) What is the name of the reservoir?

.... [1]

c) Give the six-figure grid reference for the cairn on the island.

.... [2]

4 Following the footpath, how far will you have walked in total when you reach
Fan y Big?

.... [3]

Total Marks .... / 22

Geography Skills

Geographic Information Systems

1 Which three things are needed for a GIS? Tick the correct answers.

   i) A computer or tablet ☐

   ii) A sample of rocks ☐

   iii) Instruments for measuring weather data ☐

   iv) Special GIS software ☐

   v) Digital map data ☐   [3]

2 What is a 'tour' used for in Google Earth?

_____ [1]

3 A GIS represents the real world.

a) What name is given to the different pieces of information shown in the diagram?

_____ [1]

b) What can be done to each of these pieces of information?

_____

_____

_____ [2]

c) Why might it be useful to make one of these pieces of information transparent?

_____

_____

_____ [1]

4 The features on the digital map are divided into four types. Match the words below to the statements by drawing lines between the boxes.

Polygon	These are symbols that stretch across the map in a line to show things like roads and rivers.

Line	These are symbols that represent a feature at a particular point location, e.g. a trig point.

Point	Words are used for the names of places or for the names of landscape features.

Text	These symbols cover an area and may be a regular or irregular shape.

[4]

5 In Google Earth, it is possible to zoom in and out to show the world at different scales.

a) Add the labels Global, National and Local to the correct screen shots shown below.

i) .... ii) .... iii) .... [3]

b) On a global scale, data such as cloud cover can be shown on a 'live layer'. Who would find this information useful?

.... [1]

c) On a national scale, data such as poverty levels can be shown. Who would find this information useful?

.... [1]

d) On a local scale, data such as woodland fire risk can be shown. Who would find this information useful?

.... [1]

Total Marks .... / 18

Geography Skills

Fieldwork

1 A group of students have carried out a piece of fieldwork in their local High Street. The aim of the fieldwork was to discover what types of shops/businesses were present and which sections of the High Street were busiest.

a) The High Street is about 500 metres long. A group of five students have been given the task of carrying out pedestrian counts. How should they organise themselves along the street? Explain your answer.

....

....

.... **[3]**

b) The results of the pedestrian survey collected by the students are shown below:

Student A	Student B	Student C	Student D	Student E
IIII IIII IIII II	IIII II I	IIII IIII IIII IIII II	IIII IIII II	IIII II
(I = 12 pedestrians passing each survey point over a 5-minute period)				

How many pedestrians passed each student per hour?

A .... **B** .... **C** .... **D** .... **E** .... **[5]**

c) Why are the results of this survey not likely to be very accurate? Give two reasons.

....

....

.... **[2]**

d) The students decide to plot their data on a copy of the High Street map.
How might they do this?

....

.... **[2]**

2 The map shows a group of school buildings labelled A to E. A class of Year 9 students are planning to carry out a Microclimate Survey in their school grounds.

a) What equipment will they need to record temperature and wind speed?

....

.... [2]

b) The sun rises over the school in the south-east corner and sets in the south-west corner. The wind blows most often from the south west. Building E is a very tall tower block. The points labelled X1 to X5 are possible locations for a new seating area.

Which of the five possible seating areas will be windiest? Explain why.

....

.... [2]

c) Which of the five possible seating areas will be mostly in the shade? Explain why.

....

.... [2]

3

Statement	−2 Strongly Disagree	−1 Disagree	0 Neutral	+1 Agree	+2 Strongly Agree
There is very little litter in the park.					
The park has good play facilities.					

a) The chart shows a scale being used for a local fieldwork study. What type of scale is it?

.... [1]

b) What type of data collection is this an example of?

.... [1]

c) What is the problem with this sort of data collection?

.... [1]

d) How might the 30 students doing the fieldwork best present the results of this survey?

.... [2]

Total Marks .... / 23

Mixed Test-Style Questions

1 **a)** Which of the following species of tree grow in Russia's taiga region?
Tick the correct options.

Pine	☐	Oak	☐
Palm	☐	Fir	☐
Spruce	☐	Orange	☐

☐

3 marks

b) Which type of environmental region covers most of the Middle East?

....

☐

1 mark

c) Explain why South Korea doesn't have much forest.

....

....

☐

2 marks

2 **a)** Why was the One Child Policy introduced in China?

....

....

....

☐

3 marks

b) Why do you think so many people died in the Sichuan earthquake in China?

....

....

....

☐

3 marks

3 The photograph shows the Massai in Kenya. How does the Massai's way of farming differ from cattle farming in the UK?

....

....

....

....

....

....

....

☐

5 marks

4 Several times in the Earth's history the planet has been glaciated. During a glaciation, the climate alternates between extreme cold for thousands of years and then much warmer conditions. Experts are uncertain if the last glaciation has finished or not. The graph shows the most recent part of the last glaciation.

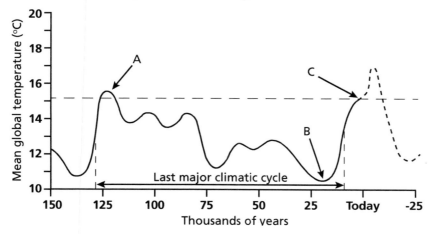

a) What names are given to the warm and cold periods during a glaciation?

Warm period _____ Cold period _____

2 marks

b) Which point on the graph (A, B or C) shows a cold period?

_____

1 mark

c) How much colder than the present day was it during this cold period?

_____

1 mark

d) Today, the global temperature appears to be rising again. This could be a natural event or it could be caused by human actions. Why might humans be responsible for this global warming?

_____

_____

2 marks

e) If it is part of a natural cycle, it is likely that the Earth will become cooler again. What problems would be caused to humans in places such as the UK if the Earth became much colder again?

_____

_____

_____

2 marks

Mixed Test-Style Questions

5 The map shows the position of two large continents millions of years ago.

a) Name the two continents.

A ....

B ....

2 marks

b) What is the fossil evidence that these two continents were once joined together?

....

....

1 mark

c) What has happened to the two continents over millions of years?

....

....

1 mark

6 The map shows the **geology** of Great Britain.

Where on the map would we find:

a) The oldest rocks?

c) Chalk?

b) The youngest rocks?

d) Rocks with lots of fossils?

4 marks

7 Sea level often changes over millions of years – sometimes it is higher than today and often it has been much lower. Thousands of years ago, it would have been possible to walk between the UK and France!

a) What has happened to sea level over the last 120 years? By how much has it changed?

....

2 marks

b) Is such a change a good thing or a bad thing? Explain your answer.

....

....

....

2 marks

8

a) What is happening to the Eurasian and North American plates?

....

1 mark

b) What type of plate boundary is found between these two plates?

....

1 mark

c) The UK is moving away from the USA and Canada by about 3 cm per year. How much further apart will they be in:

i) 1000 years? .... **ii)** 1 000 000 years? ....

2 marks

d) Iceland is a volcanic island which is located on top of the plate boundary. Which of the following statements is true? Tick the correct option.

i) Iceland is getting smaller.

ii) Iceland is getting larger.

iii) Iceland is staying the same size.

1 mark

Mixed Test-Style Questions

9 The 2004 Asian tsunami was an example of a devastating natural disaster caused by an earthquake. It created a powerful wave that was up to 30 metres high when it hit the coast of many South East Asian countries.

a) Give two examples of the kinds of problem caused by such waves:

i) People ....

ii) Homes ....

2 marks

b) Many countries now have tsunami warning systems that are activated whenever there is a large earthquake. What should people do when the warning system goes off?

....

....

1 mark

10 a) What type of rock is this? Tick the corect option.

Sedimentary ☐

Metamorphic ☐

Igneous ☐

1 mark

b) Describe how it formed.

....

....

....

....

5 marks

c) This is a picture of slate used on a roof. Why is it good to use for roof tiles?

....

....

....

....

☐ 4 marks

11 The photograph shows a section of soil.

A →

← B

C

a) Name A ....

☐ 1 mark

b) What happens at B to influence the characteristics of the soil?

....

....

....

☐ 3 marks

c) Name four factors that affect how quickly the soil develops at C.

....

....

....

☐ 4 marks

Mixed Test-Style Questions

12 Terracing is a strategy that farmers use to prevent soil erosion. With the aid of a diagram, explain how terracing achieves this.

....

....

....

....

....

5 marks

13 In general, it gets colder as you move from the equator to the poles.

North Pole
Arctic Circle
60° N
Sun's rays
Tropic of Cancer
Equator
Tropic of Capricorn
60° S
South Pole
Antarctic Circle

Give two reasons to explain why the energy from the sun is strongest at the equator and weakest at the poles.

1 ....

....

2 ....

....

4 marks

14 Match the type of climate to the correct temperature and rainfall characteristics by drawing lines between the boxes.

Temperate climate
Desert climate
Tropical climate
Polar climate

Hot all year round
Hot all year round, high total rainfall
Warm in summer, cool in winter
Very low total rainfall, very cold all year round

4 marks

15 Describe two ways in which the climate at the top of a mountain range will be different to that of the surrounding lowland areas.

....

....

....

2 marks

16 This image is an oblique aerial photograph of part of the River Amazon.

a) Name the landforms shown.

....

1 mark

b) Name the process that happens on the outside of the river bend.

....

1 mark

c) Explain what will eventually happen to the bends in the river.

....

....

....

4 marks

d) Name the landform left behind.

....

1 mark

17 Insert the correct letters into the boxes to match the terms to their definitions.

A migration   **B** emigrants   **C** immigrants
D illegal immigrants **E** economic migrants **F** refugees

	The people arriving in a new country are called ....
	If people enter a country without permission, they are referred to as ....
	The people choosing to leave a country are known as ....
	The majority of people who move are .... , seeking higher paid work and a better life.
	The process of moving between countries is known as ....
	If people are forced to leave a country because of famine, war or a natural disaster, they become ....

6 marks

Mixed Test-Style Questions

18 The population of Country X is 50 million people.

The number of births in Country X is 800 000 babies per year.

The number of deaths per year in Country X is 600 000 people per year.

The number of immigrants into Country X is 500 000 people per year.

The number of emigrants from Country X is 300 000 people per year.

a) What is the natural increase in Country X?

.... 1 mark

b) What is the increase due to migration in Country X?

.... 1 mark

c) Using the data above, estimate the population of Country X in 10 years' time.

.... 1 mark

d) If the government of Country X reduces immigration by half, what effect will this have on total population change each year?

....

.... 2 marks

19 The civil war in Syria has meant that over two million people have become refugees and have fled to neighbouring countries such as Jordan, Egypt and Turkey to escape the war. Most have no money and nowhere to stay.

Describe two problems that these refugees cause for the countries that they flee to.

....

....

....

.... 2 marks

20 Family planning campaigns give people advice about how many children they should have. In China, the government advised people to have fewer children – preferably only one child per family. In Italy and France, people were encouraged to have more children.

Why do countries give such different advice?

....

....

....

....

2 marks

21 Look carefully at these photographs showing different views of housing in towns and cities in the UK. Make a list of the characteristics of each type of housing.

a)	b)

6 marks

Mixed Test-Style Questions

22 For each image say how it benefits people, the planet and helps cities to prosper.

People

Planet

Profit

People

Planet

Profit

People

Planet

Profit

9 marks

23 Study the data table and answer the questions.

	Kenya	Saudi Arabia	China
	2012	2012	2012
GDP (USD)	40 billion	711 billion	8.2 trillion
GNI per person	943	25,136	6,091
Adult literacy rate	72 (2007)	86.5 (2010)	95 (2010)
Life Expectancy	57.7	74.1	73.7
Human Development Index (Rank)	0.519 (145)	0.782 (57)	0.699 (101)

a) Which country generated the most income in 2012? .... 1 mark

b) i) Which country had the highest GNI per person in 2012? .... 1 mark

ii) Why isn't it the same country as in part **a)**? ....
.... 2 marks

c) Suggest reasons for the differences in HDI between the three countries.

....
....
....
.... 3 marks

24 The people below all work in the tertiary sector providing a service to other people or organisations. Explain two ways that we might divide these jobs into two separate groups.

- A lawyer defending people in court.
- A street cleaner picking up litter.
- A vet looking after sick animals.
- A carer helping in an old people's nursing home.
- A teacher working in a secondary school.

....
....
....
.... 2 marks

Mixed Test-Style Questions

25 Many companies that are based in the USA and other HICs are multinational companies. This means that they have factories and offices in many different countries. Apple is a global company that makes the iPhone and the iPad. These products are designed in the USA, where some parts are made. Other parts come from South Korea, Japan, Switzerland and also China, where they are assembled and shipped to the USA ready for sale.

Give two reasons why companies such as Apple organise their business in this way.

3 marks

26 Imagine that you were a poor farmer living on the edge of the Amazon rainforest. You are struggling to survive and feed your family. A Canadian timber company announces that it has a licence from the Brazilian government to cut down a large part of the forest close to where you live.

a) Why might you be very excited by the news about the timber company?

1 mark

b) Why might the timber company be very pleased that they have permission to cut down trees?

1 mark

c) Why might the Brazilian government have been pleased to have given the company a licence?

1 mark

d) Why might people in the UK and other countries not be pleased to hear about this news?

1 mark

27 Which two of the following are fossil fuels? Tick the correct options.

a) Coal ☐

b) Wood ☐

c) Electricity ☐

d) Nuclear ☐

e) Natural gas ☐

f) Wind ☐

☐ 2 marks

28 Study the data shown below.

The data shows millions of tonnes of fish reared on fish farms (2001–2010).

2001	2002	2003	2004	2005	2006	2007	2008	2009	2010
34	36	39	42	44	47	49	53	55	59

a) Describe, using the data, how the amount of fish reared on fish farms has changed over the ten years shown.

....

....

....

....

☐ 3 marks

b) Explain why more fish are being reared in fish farms and fewer wild fish are being caught each year.

....

....

....

☐ 3 marks

29 Study the Ordnance Survey map below, and the photograph.

a) This photograph was taken at 705131. Which direction was the photographer facing?

1 mark

b) What is the name of the lake in the photograph?

1 mark

c) How far away is the lake from the photographer? ....

2 marks

d) What is the highest point on the map? ....

1 mark

e) Is there a footpath around the lake? ....

1 mark

f) i) What type of landform is the lake part of? ....

1 mark

ii) What information does the map give to help you come to this conclusion?

....

....

....

3 marks

30 Digital maps can now be carried by anyone who has a smartphone or a sat nav fitted to their car.

a) Give one advantage of carrying digital maps rather than paper maps.

....

1 mark

b) If you are travelling, what three pieces of information provided on the digital map help you get to your destination?

....

3 marks

c) How does the system know your current location?

....

1 mark

Mixed Test-Style Questions

31 Study the questionnaire below.

Fieldwork Questionnaire	
1.	What is your name? ....
2.	What is your age? 0 – 15 [ ] 15 – 35 [ ] 35 – 55 [ ] 55 and over [ ]
3.	What do you like about this town? ....

a) It is better if questionnaires are anonymous – what needs to be changed to make it anonymous?

....

1 mark

b) What is the problem with the way that question 2 has been written? How would you improve it?

....

....

....

....

2 mark

c) Look at questions 2 and 3. Which is an open question and which is a closed question?

Question 2 ....   Question 3 ....

2 mark

32 Students have collected fieldwork data about the number of tourists visiting different parts of their local town. They have used the data to create this map.

Pedestrian Density Map
(Number of people per hour)

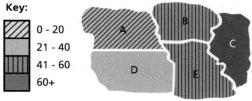

Key:
- 0 - 20
- 21 - 40
- 41 - 60
- 60+

a) What type of map have they chosen to represent the data?

....

1 mark

b) i) Which area of town received the fewest tourists?

....

1 marks

ii) Why can't we tell exactly how many people visited this area?

....

1 mark

Answers

Pages 148–153 Place Knowledge

Page 148: Location Knowledge – Russia

1. a) i) Finland ii) Ukraine iii) Kazakhstan
      iv) Mongolia v) China   [5]
   b) vi) St Petersburg vii) Moscow
      viii) Omsk ix) Vladivostok   [4]
   c) Volga River   [1]
2. a) Region of grassland plains; south of
      taiga; dry climate; chernozem soil; soil
      is fertile; good for agriculture.
      (Any 2 for [2])
   b) Region of coniferous trees; e.g. pine, fir,
      spruce; covers roughly 60% of Russia.
      (Any 2 for [2])
   c) In far north of Russia; temperatures can
      drop to -50°C; trees cannot grow; ground
      is frozen all year round/permafrost.
      (Any 2 for [2])

Page 149: Location Knowledge – China

1. a) i) Pakistan ii) Nepal iii) Myanmar
      iv) Vietnam v) North Korea
      vi) Mongolia   [6]
   b) vii) Beijing viii) Tianjin
      ix) Chongqing x) Shanghai   [4]
   c) A = Yellow River; B = Yangtze River [2]
2. a) Introduced in 1979; to control rapidly
      growing population; reduced number of
      births; by 400 million between 1979 and
      2009. **(Any 2 points for [2])**
   b) Over 150 Chinese cities have population
      of at least 1 million; largest city is
      Chongqing; Chongqing has nearly
      29 million people; second largest city
      is Shanghai; capital Beijing is third
      largest; Tianjin is fourth largest.
      (Any 3 points for [3])

Page 150: Location Knowledge – India

1. a) i) Pakistan ii) Bangladesh
      iii) Myanmar iv) Nepal v) China [5]
   b) River Ganges   [1]
   c) vi) Delhi vii) Mumbai
      viii) Bangalore ix) Chennai   [4]
2. Major Indian industries include motor
   vehicles/ship building/telecommunications/
   software/computers/chemicals; India will be
   the world's third largest economy by 2025;
   wages have doubled since 2000; many
   Indians live on less than $1.25 a day. **(Any 2
   points for [2])**

Page 151: Location Knowledge – The Middle East

1. a) i) Turkey ii) Syria iii) Jordan
      iv) Saudi Arabia v) Yemen vi) UAE
      vii) Oman viii) Iran ix) Iraq [9]
   b) **In any order:** Egypt; Lebanon;
      Kuwait; Bahrain; Cyprus; Israel;
      Qatar; Palestine   [8]
   c) x) Cairo xi) Baghdad xii) Tehran [3]
2. Nile; Euphrates; Tigris   [3]
3. Exporting oil   [1]

Page 152: Africa and Asia Compared – Kenya

1. a) i) South Sudan ii) Uganda
      iii) Tanzania iv) Somalia
      v) Ethiopia   [5]
   b) vi) Lake Turkana vii) Lake Victoria [2]
   c) viii) Nairobi ix) Mombasa   [2]
2. Great Rift Valley runs through west Kenya;
   It is formed from the splitting of the
   African tectonic plate; The valley has been
   partially filled by lakes.   [3]
3. Kenya has a young population; Average
   age is 18; 6% are over 55; over 60% are
   under 25.   [4]

**Page 153: Africa and Asia Compared –
South Korea**

1. a) i) China ii) Japan iii) North Korea [3]
    b) iv) Seoul v) Incheon vi) Busan
       vii) Daegu [4]
2. Nakdong River; Han River [2]
3. Samsung; Daewoo; Hyundai; LG; Kia;
    Ssangyong. **(Any four for [4])**
4. No limits/additional costs on imports/
    exports; between the EU and South
    Korea. [2]

Pages 154–155 Geological Timescale

1. a) Sedimentary rock. [1]
    b) Fossils. [1]
    c) The rocks in layer 4 are likely to be the
       oldest [1] as the newest layers of sand
       and mud are deposited on top of the
       older layers. [1]
2. a) 183 million years. [1]
    b) The Cretaceous period. [1]
    c) Chalk. [1]
    d) There are fossils of creatures that lived
       in tropical seas trapped in the chalk. [1]
    e) The dinosaurs. [1]
    f) They became extinct (died out). [1]

3.

4.6 billion years ago	The time when humans appeared on Earth.
350 million years ago	The time when the Earth was first formed.
2.3 million years ago	The time when reptiles and flying insects first appeared.
3.5 billion years ago	The time when the first life appeared on Earth in the oceans.

(1 mark per correct answer) [4]

4. a) Africa. [1]
    b) Evolution – the process by which species
       change over time. [1]

c) As humans evolved, they developed
   larger brains than their ancestors [1] and
   they became taller. [1]
d) By hunting animals [1] and picking fruit,
   nuts and berries. [1]
e) Making fire [1] and using tools. [1]

Pages 156–157 Plate Tectonics

1.

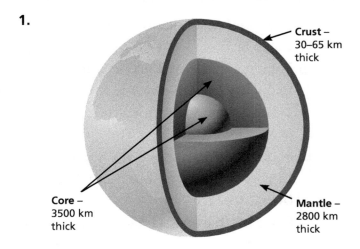

Crust – 30–65 km thick

Core – 3500 km thick

Mantle – 2800 km thick

**(1 mark per correct thickness and 1 mark
per correct label)** [6]

2.

Crustal plates	A plate that is very thick with a mountain range lying on top.
Plate boundary	A plate that has very thin crust with an ocean lying on top.
Oceanic crust	The line along which two crustal plates meet.
Continental crust	The individual sections of the Earth's crust.

(1 mark per correct answer) [4]

3. E – D – A – F – C – B
    (1 mark per correct answer) [6]
4. a) A conservative boundary. [1]
    b) iii [1]
    c) An earthquake. [1]
5. a) Point A = Focus   Point B = Epicentre [2]

b) The house at X **[1]** as this is where the shock waves are most powerful and strike first. **[1]**

c) Earthquakes cause the ground to crack and this damages gas pipes and electrical cables, **[1]** which leads to fires breaking out. **[1]**

d) A tsunami. **[1]**

Pages 158–159 **Rocks and Geology**

1. a) Your diagram must clearly show big gaps between the minerals in the porous rock.

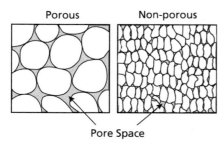

Porous   Non-porous

Pore Space

[1] per correct diagram; [1] for label

Labelling diagrams always makes it easier to show what you mean.

b) i) Porous **[1]**
ii) Porous **[1]**
iii) Non-porous **[1]**
iv) Porous **[1]**
v) Non-porous **[1]**
vi) Non-porous **[1]**

2. Sedimentary rocks are porous, which makes them easier to erode and weather. **[1]** Sedimentary rocks are formed from the remains of dead organisms and deposits from weathered and eroded older rocks. **[1]**

3. a) Sedimentary rocks **[1]**
Reason: They are formed from the particles of other rock or organic matter **[1]** and they may contain fossils. **[1]**

b) Oxidation **[1]**
Reason: Oxidation is a form of chemical weathering **[1]** whereas the others are physical weathering processes. **[1]**

c) Sandstone **[1]**
Reason: Sandstone is a sedimentary rock **[1]**; the other two are metamorphic. **[1]**

d) Basalt **[1]**
Reason: Basalt is an igneous rock **[1]**; the other two are sedimentary rocks. **[1]**

It is really important that you have used the key words in your reasons.

4. The remains of plants and animals **[1]** became trapped between layers of sediment **[1]** when the rock was formed. **[1]**

Pages 160–161 **Weathering and Soil**

1.

Chemical weathering	Layers of rock flake off due to expansion and contradiction
Freeze-thaw weathering	Rocks are broken down by plants and animals
Onion-skin weathering	Weak acid dissolves rock
Biological weathering	Pieces of rock break off due to expansion

(1 mark per correct answer) **[4]**

2. a) i) B, D, C, A **[2]**
ii) Chemical weathering **[1]**
b) i) A, D, C, B **[2]**
ii) Onion-skin weathering **[1]**
c) i) D, C, A, B **[2]**
ii) Biological weathering **[1]**
d) i) B, A, D, C **[2]**
ii) Freeze-thaw weathering **[1]**

3. a) Dead plants = ✓, Dead animals = ✓, Minerals = ✓, Water = ✓, Air = ✓, Worms = ✗ **[6]**

b)

[4]

4.

B	Parent material: the rock type that the soil is formed from.
O	Sub soil where weathered rock is becoming part of the soil
A	Surface layer consisting of surface layers and twigs
R	Top soil rich in nutrients, minerals and humus
C	Bedrock, solid rock that cannot be dug out by hand.

(1 mark per correct answer) [5]

Pages 162–163 **Weather and Climate**

1. *90% – Humidity*
15 mm – Rainfall
6°C – Temperature
North west – Wind direction
1012 mb – Air pressure
30 mph – Wind speed [6]

2. Hail ⬭Rain Snow [3]

3. Minimum temperature – C
Temperature range – A
Maximum temperature – B [3]

4. The weather forecast for Wales is warmer [1] at 20°C compared to 10°C for Scotland. [1] The weather forecast for Scotland gives cloud and rain [1] compared to sunny intervals for Wales. [1]

5. When air rises, the air pressure **decreases** and when air sinks, the air pressure

increases. Air moves from areas of **high** pressure to areas of **low** pressure. [4]

6. **a)** 3 **b)** 1 **c)** 4 **d)** 2 **e)** 5 [5]

7. **[5]** for accurate plotting of rainfall data as a bar chart and **[5]** for accurate plotting of temperature data as a line graph. **[10]**

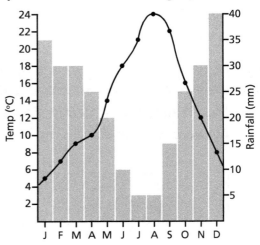

Pages 164–165 **Glaciation**

1. **a)** 4 **b)** 2 **c)** 1 **d)** 3 [4]

2.

Truncated spur   U-shaped valley

Ribbon lake [3]

3. **a)** 6 **b)** 3 **c)** 4 **d)** 2 **e)** 5
f) 7 **g)** 1 [7]

4. **The tweet should include ideas such as:** dramatic scenery; attracts large number of tourists; **You may also have included:** ideas that honeypot sites might not be sustainable; and generate conflict.
[1] for each point up to a maximum of [2]

5. **There is no right or wrong answer to the conflict matrix. Ask yourself this question: can you give an example and reason for each of your decisions?** [2]

6. **Ideas you could include:** being considerate of other users, [1] buy local produce, [1] stick to designated paths, [1] observe speed limits, [1] take litter home with you. [1]

1. The river flows over different types of rock. [1] Softer rock types erode more easily than harder rock types. [1] The softer rock underneath the harder rock is undercut [1] leaving an overhang. [1] Eventually the overhang collapses into the plunge pool [1] and the waterfall retreats upstream. [1]

2. Hydraulic action in rivers occurs as the river flows along the river bank, [1] whereas at the coast, hydraulic action is caused when waves break on cliff faces. [1]

3. Because they erode at different speeds, [1] which leads to different types of landforms. [1] For example at the coast bays and headlands [1] are formed because of different rates of erosion. [1] Another example would be waterfalls. [1]
    (Any 3 for [3])

4. Building towns and cities contributes to flooding by removing trees and other plants [1] that help to slow down [1] how quickly water gets into rivers. [1] **OR** Building towns and cities contributes to flooding by increasing the amount of impermeable land [1] that helps speed up [1] how quickly water gets into rivers. [1]

5. Constructive waves have low energy, [1] which means they deposit sediment [1] that they carry as they break [1] on the beach. The swash is more powerful than the backwash. [1]

6. Hard engineering helps protect communities [1] by reflecting, absorbing and dissipating wave energy and therefore slowing the rate of coastal erosion. [1] Hard engineering also helps to keep beaches in place [1] by reducing the effects of longshore drift. [1]

7. **For:** Environmentalists, because it allows nature to take its course [1] and allows wetlands to develop [1] which are important for coastal ecosystems and biodiversity. [1]
    Against: Residents, because they will lose their homes and be forced to move. They will not be able to sell their homes. [1] Some residents will be farmers [1] and will find it difficult to make a living because they will not be able to use their land any more. [1]

1. 1 Grow food **or** Plants produce oxygen. [1]
    2 Build using stone **or** Use water from rivers to drink. [1]
    3 Enjoy the outdoors **or** Experience nature and the natural environment. [1]
    4 Get metals and minerals from rocks. [1]

2. Environments with low rain fall and extreme environments are 'fragile'. [2]

3.

Factory produces pollution and CO_2

Trees and other plants photosynthesise capturing CO_2

There are millions of trees in the rainforest.

Each tree stores carbon taken from the air.

Carbon is trapped inside the trees until they are burnt.

[5]

4.

Reafforestation	Creating protected areas of rainforest
Conservation	Planting crops amongst the trees to prevent soil erosion
Agro-forestry	Monitor illegal deforestation and disruptions to indigenous people.
Satellite photography	Planting trees to replace the ones cut down

(1 mark per correct answer) [4]

5. Increasing population is leading to overpopulation; The savannah's carrying capacity is quite low; The savannah is found in dry areas so can suffer from drought. **[3]**

6. Reduce grazing – Gives grassland and trees time to recover so soil is not lost when plants and trees die. **[1]**

   'Magic stones' – Trap water and soil after rain and prevents soil from being washed away. **[1]**

   Planting trees – The roots of the trees help to bind the soil together. The trees provide shelter from the wind and prevent soil being blown away. **[1]**

   Drought-resistant plants – Keep growing even when there is little rainfall. Help to provide shelter to prevent soil from blowing away. **[1]**

   Terracing – Helps to trap water and soil after it has rained. Makes farming on hillsides much easier. **[1]**

Pages 170–171 **Population**

1. a) Seven billion and two hundred and fifty million people **[1]**
   b) 34% **[1]**

2. a) It has continued to decline since 1970. **[1]**
   b) China started off with around 5.5 births per woman in 1970. This fell rapidly to 2.7 by 1980 **[1]** and has continued to decline slowly to around 1.7 by 2010. **[1]** In Indonesia, there were around 5.6 births per woman in 1970. There was a steady decline to around 2.5 by 2000 **[1]** and it has remained at the same level since that date. **[1]**
   c) The number of babies being born in most countries is declining **[1]** and this means that population growth will slow down. **[1]**

3. Marshland – Sparse; Fertile land – Dense; Land covered by ice – Sparse; Desert – Sparse; Flat land – Dense **[5]**

4. a) South Korea, UK, Egypt, Peru, Russia **[1]**
   b)

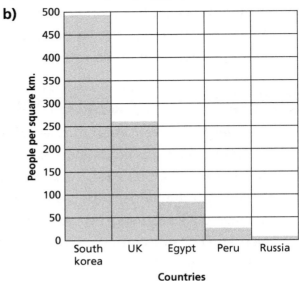

(1 mark per country plotted accurately and in correct order.) **[5]**

5. Poverty results in people having a poor diet or insufficient food, **[1]** which leads to illness and/or death. **[1]**

Pages 172–173 **Urbanisation**

1. **Some of the possible reasons you may have considered include:**
   a) Paid employment **[1]**
      Education **[1]**
      Access to healthcare **[1]**
   b) Fewer jobs in farming **[1]**
      Drought **[1]**
      Loss of land **[1]**
   c) Family ties to area **[1]**
      Only one or two members of the family can move **[1]**
      Have no contacts in the city **[1]**

2. **Any suitable problem for [1], with two suitable solutions [2]. For example:**
   Problem: Too many people competing for the same road space. **[1]**
   Solutions: Segregating road users; **[1]** making cycle lanes bigger and easier to use. **[1]**
   Problem: Poor public transport services; **[1]** either not enough buses for the number of passengers

or not a frequent enough service.

Solution: Prioritise buses and make sure no other vehicles use bus lanes. [1] Encourage bus companies to put on more services by paying them for distances travelled not number of passengers carried. [1]

3. a) **You are likely to have scored the favela very low on the environmental quality survey and have probably given it a negative score. The important part of this task is to think about what this might mean.** [2]

b) A poor quality environment, [1] which means that people will find it difficult to move around [1] because of poor roads and alleyways. [1]

c) People often have little money [1] and cannot afford to live in more expensive places. [1] People who have lived here a long time [1] have a strong sense of community [1] and do not want to live elsewhere. [1] People are likely to be earning only a small wage [1] and cannot afford to move. [1]

(Any three points for [3])

Pages 174–175 Development

1. a) **Social Indicators** – Literacy rate; infant mortality rate; life expectancy

Economic Indicators – GDP per capita; Gross Domestic Product; primary industries; secondary industries; tertiary industries. [8]

b) Literacy rate – up; infant mortality rate – down; Life expectancy – up; GDP per capita – up; Gross Domestic Product – up; Primary industries – down; Secondary industries–up; teritary industries – up. [8]

2. a) 3 or 4 b) 4 or 3 c) 2 d) 1 [4]

3. Life expectancy; number of years at school; GNI per capita; adult literacy [4]

4. A Environment is protected by traditional farming practices. Environmental [1]

B The farmer is paid a fair price. Economic [1]

C Fair trade dividend goes to community groups. Economic and Social [1]

D Community groups hold meetings to discuss their needs. Social [1]

E People are elected to represent their communities. Social [1]

F Farmers can grow crops in traditional ways which protect the environment. Social and Environmental [1]

G Communities choose what is best for them. Social, Environmental and Economic (i.e. middle segment) [1]

H Products have a stable price. Economic [1]

I Communities can put in place long-term plans. Social, Environmental and Economic [1]

Pages 176–177 Economic Activity

1.

Production	is the selling and buying of goods in shops.
Distribution	is the making of goods in factories and workshops.
Consumption	is the transport of goods from factories to ~~sh~~

(1 mark per correct li

2. I work on a farm driv wheat. – Primary
I work in a factory ma
I put the motor into e
Secondary
I work in a jewellery workshop making beautiful bracelets. – Secondary
I work in an estate agents helping people buy and sell their homes. – Tertiary [4]

3. a) To build on
   b) To make their products
   c) To power the factory
   d) To make their products
   e) To move products to market [5]
4. Country A is an HIC and Country B is an LIC. [2]
5. Orange [1]
6. a) Mechanised
   b) Pastoral
   c) Arable
   d) Organic [4]

Pages 178–179 Natural Resources

1. Coal = Natural   Wood = Natural
   Glass = Man-made   Plastic = Man-made
   Marble = Natural   Water = Natural [6]
2. a) False
   b) True
   c) False [3]
3. a) This not only replaces the cut tree but
      also increases the number of trees
      available for future generations. [1] This
      is an example of sustainable forestry. [1]

   When a question asks you to include a
   particular word or phrase, make sure you
   include it in your answer.

   b) You would plant coniferous trees [1] as
      these grow quite quickly taking 20–30
      years to reach full size. [1]
4. a) Non-renewable means that a resource
      cannot be replaced by humans and will
      eventually run out. [1]
      rink cans – non-renewable; Plastic
      ottles – non-renewable; Glass bottles –
      n-renewable; Paper products –
      ewable resource. [4]
   c) It is a way of extending the life of the
      resource. [1]
   d) It reduces the amount of waste that
      has to be disposed of in waste tips or
      incinerators. [1]

Pages 180–181 Ordnance Survey Maps

1. a) Public toilet. [1]
   b) North east. [1]
   c) 2.7 km [2] 2.5 or 2.8 km. [1]
   d) 440 m [2]
2. a) Pen y Fan 012215; [2] 886 m [1]
   b) Cribyn 023213; [2] 795 m [1]
   c) Fan y Big 036206; [2] 719 m [1]
3. a) 0219 [1]
   b) Neuadd Reservoir [1]
   c) 028192 [2]
4. 6.2 km [3]

Pages 182–183 Geographic Information Systems

1. i) A computer or tablet
   iv) Special GIS software
   v) Digital map data [3]
2. It is a way of recording a journey from one
   location to another. [1]
3. a) Layers. [1]
   b) The layers can be switched on [1] or
      switched off if not needed. [1]
   c) It can be useful to make a layer
      transparent to see the relationship
      between two different layers. [1]

4.

Polygon	These are symbols that stretch across the map in a line to show things like roads and rivers.
Line	These are symbols that represent a feature at a particular point location e.g. a trig point.
Point	Words are used for the names of places or for the names of landscape features.
Text	These symbols cover an area and may be a regular or irregular shape.

(1 mark per correct answer) [4]

5. a) i) National ii) Global iii) Local [3]
   b) A person studying the weather or trying to make a weather forecast. [1]
   c) Government organisations or charities. [1]
   d) Local authorities and emergency services. [1]

Pages 184–185 Fieldwork

1. a) The students should organise themselves in a systematic way [1] so that they are spaced out an equal distance; [1] in this case about every 100 metres. [1]
   b) A = 168 B = 84 C = 216
      D = 120 E = 72 [5]
   c) The students are spaced out a long way apart [1] and the survey may happen at a very busy or a very quiet time that is not typical. [1]
   d) The students could use proportional symbols, e.g. an image of a pedestrian [1] or they could draw a bar to scale at each location in the survey. [1]
2. a) A thermometer (to record temperature) [1] and an anemometer (to record wind speed). [1]
   b) X2 is likely to be the windiest (X4 will also be windy). [1] Both these sites are exposed to the wind blowing from the south west. [1]
   c) X4 and X5 will be in the shade for much of the time [1] owing to the tall building labelled E. [1]
3. a) This is a bi-polar scale. [1]
   b) Perception – finding out what people think about something. [1]
   c) People's opinions can vary for many different reasons and some people may be biased. [1]
   d) Convert it to percentages [1] and present it as a pie chart. [1]

Pages 186–201 Mixed Test-Style Questions

1. a) Pine; Fir; Spruce. [3]
   b) Desert. [1]
   c) Forest doesn't grow in mountainous regions. [1] Much of South Korea's forest has been cut down. [1]
2. a) To reduce the size of China's population. [1] The population was growing rapidly. [1] There was concern that China wouldn't be able to produce enough food, jobs, housing, schools, doctors for so many people. [1]
   b) A large population makes it likely that large numbers will be killed. [1] Sichuan is a poor area with weak houses [1] built on steep, unstable slopes. [1]
3. Nomadic pastoralism, [1] which means moving their herds [1] in search of water and pasture. [1] In the UK, cattle farmers stay in the same place, [1] fertiliser/irrigation/cattle feed are available. [1]
4. a) Warm period = Interglacial [1]
      Cold period = Glacial [1]
   b) Point B [1]
   c) It was about 4 to 5 degrees colder than present-day global average temperature. [1]
   d) Humans cause air pollution [1] and many of these gases trap heat in the atmosphere. [1]
   e) If another glacial period started, it would be impossible to live in the UK as ice sheets would expand and cover the land. [1] Homes and property would be destroyed and people would have to move further south. [1]
5. a) A = South America B = Africa [2]
   b) Fossils of the same creatures are found in rocks on both continents. [1]
   c) The two continents have gradually moved apart and the Atlantic Ocean has formed in between. [1]

6. a) The oldest rocks – B
    b) The youngest rocks – A
    c) Chalk – A
    d) Rocks with lots of fossils – A   **[4]**
7. a) The sea level has gradually risen **[1]** by
        20 cm **[1]**
    b) Sea level rise is a bad thing **[1]** as it
        increases the risk of flooding along the
        coast, particularly where the land is very
        low and flat. **[1]**
8. a) The Eurasian and North American plates
        are moving away from each other.   **[1]**
    b) A constructive plate boundary.   **[1]**
    c) i)   30 metres   **[1]**
        ii) 30 000 metres or 30 km   **[1]**
    d) ii)   **[1]**
9. a) i)   Many people are likely to be killed
            or injured.   **[1]**
        ii) Homes will be damaged or
            destroyed.   **[1]**
    b) If the tsunami warning goes off, people
        should stop what they are doing and
        travel away from the coast, preferably
        to high ground. If this is not possible
        they should seek shelter in a tall, strong
        building.   **[1]**
10. a) Metamorphic.   **[1]**
    b) Formed when heat and pressure cause
        rocks to change. **[1]** Tectonic movements
        [1] cause rocks to get closer to the hot
        magma **[1]** Heat changes the chemicals
        in the rocks. **[1]** Minerals are arranged in
        layers. **[1]**
    c) The slate is non-porous **[1]** so rainwater
        can run off the surface easily. **[1]** It is less
        susceptible to weathering **[1]** and so will
        last a long time. **[1]** It forms in layers, **[1]**
        which makes it easy to cut into tiles. **[1]**
        (Any 4 points for [4])
11. a) O horizon.   **[1]**
    b) Leaves drop from the plants, **[1]** they lie
        on the top of the soil **[1]** and begin to
        decompose **[1]** forming a humus layer.

[1] Over time the remains become part
of the soil. **[1] (Any 3 ideas for [3])**
    c) **Any four of the following:** climate,
        organisms, parent material, relief, time. **[4]**
12. **Your diagram should show steps in the
    side of a hill with walls at the edge. Your
    annotations should describe how the
    terrace works.**
    Terracing helps prevent soil erosion by
    creating flat fields **[1]** that stop soil from
    being washed away by the rain. **[1]** Walls
    trap running water and soil. **[1]** Small fields
    [1] surrounded by walls also help reduce
    wind erosion. **[1]**
13. In equatorial areas (between the Tropic of
    Cancer and the Tropic of Capricorn) the sun
    is overhead for the majority of the year
    [1] and its energy passes through a narrow
    part of the atmosphere.   **[1]**
    In polar areas, the sun's energy passes
    through a thicker layer of atmosphere. **[1]**
    It also strikes the Earth at a low angle and
    some energy is lost by reflection back into
    space.   **[1]**
14.

Temperate climate	Hot all year round
Desert climate	Hot all year round, high total rainfall
Tropical climate	Warm in summer, cool in winter
Polar climate	Very low total rainfall, very cold all year round

(1 mark per correct answer)   **[4]**
15. The climate at the top of the mountain
    range will be cooler/colder **[1]** and
    wetter/more rain/more snow **[1]** than the
    surrounding lowland areas.
16. a) Meanders.   **[1]**
    b) Erosion.   **[1]**
    c) Water in the river will take the shortest
        route **[1]** so water in the bend will start
        to slow down. **[1]** Silt will build up at

each end of the bend. **[1]** Eventually the bend will be completely cut off from the main course of the river. **[1]**

d) Ox-bow lake. **[1]**

17. C – D – B – E – A – F **[6]**

18. a) 200 000 people per year **[1]**
    b) 200 000 people per year **[1]**
    c) 54 million **[1]**
    d) Total annual population change will be reduced from 400 000 people **[1]** to 150 000 people. **[1]**

19. The refugees cause problems because they need to be provided with food and shelter **[1]** and the countries are unable to provide these things for the large numbers of refugees arriving each year. **[1]**

20. They give different advice because each country is trying to deal with a different problem. **[1]** In some countries, there are too many babies being born and in other countries there is a drop in the number of babies being born. **[1]**

21. **Your answers need to focus on the housing. Some suggestions include:**
    a) Detached and semi-detached houses. **[1]** Front and back gardens. **[1]** Housing organised in crescents, cul-de-sacs. **[1]** Trees and bushes planted in open areas. **[1] (Any 3 points for [3])**
    b) Mixture of high and low rise flats. **[1]** High density – many families in each block. **[1]** Trees suggest that there might be a park at the bottom of the flats. **[1]** Space shared with lots of other people. **[1] (Any 3 points for [3])**

22. **Ideas like these, 1 mark for each suggestion up to a maximum of [9]. Try not to repeat the same reasons for different strategies.**
    a) (Boris) Bikes: People – get fitter; Planet – fewer cars being used; Profit – earns money as the bikes are rented. **[3]**
    b) Electric cars: People – quieter; cause less noise pollution; Planet – fewer

greenhouse gas emissions; Profit – new industries are developed to supply the batteries for the cars. **[3]**

c) Solar panels: People – can make their own electricity from their roofs; Planet – more renewable sources of electricity being used; Profit – government gives grants (small amounts of money) to people to pay for the panels. **[3]**

23. a) China **[1]**
    b) i) Saudi Arabia **[1]**
       ii) Bigger population in China. **[1]** Over 1.3 billion people live in China. **[1]**

    You need to include data about China's population size.

    c) **There are lots of ways to answer this question. Your answer should refer to all three countries and should include figures from the table. The challenge is to suggest why China has a lower HDI than Saudi Arabia. Ideas might include:** – Kenya has much lower indicators overall **[1]** China is lower than Saudi Arabia **[1]** as GNI per person is less than a quarter. **[1]**

24. The list of people can be divided into two groups on the basis of skills/qualifications, i.e. highly qualified and skilled versus low qualification and skills, **[1]** and what each person is paid, i.e. high salary and low paid workers. **[1]**

25. Companies such as Apple need to use HICs for research and development as this is where the people have the skills **[1]** but they need to use other countries, particularly NICs, for high-tech components **[1]** and countries where labour is cheap, such as China, for assembly. **[1]**

26. a) It provides the opportunity to get paid work. **[1]**
    b) It gives them an opportunity to sell timber and make a profit. **[1]**

c) It creates an opportunity to export timber and make money for the country through export taxes. [1]

d) Because of the destruction of part of the rainforest as they may be concerned about the loss of habitat and wildlife. [1]

27. Coal; natural gas. [2]

28. a) In 2001, 34 million tonnes of fish were reared on fish farms. [1] This has increased every year [1] and by 2010, 59 million tonnes of fish were reared on fish farms. [1]

b) In many seas and oceans there is overfishing, [1] which means that there are fewer and fewer fish left to breed and keep the fish stocks going. [1] The only alternative then is to artificially rear fish on fish farms to provide food. [1]

29. a) North east [1]

b) Llyn y Gadair [1]

c) 500 m [2]

d) 893 m [1]

e) Yes [1]

f) i) Corrie [1]

ii) Contour lines are close together/very steep; [1] contour lines in a crescent shape suggests armchair-shaped landform; [1] small round lake in the bottom. [1]

30. a) Digital maps are more convenient as they don't take up lots of space; it is easy to find a location using the search facility; it is easy to update. (Any 1 for [1])

b) Direction, time to destination and distance to destination. [3]

c) The sat nav system uses an in-built GPS to locate your position on the digital map. [1]

31. a) The first question needs to be removed. [1]

b) Question 2 has an overlap in the categories used so, for example, a 15-year-old person would fit into two different categories. [1] It can be improved by changing the categories so that they don't overlap, e.g. 0–15, 16–35. [1]

c) Question 2 = Closed
Question 3 = Open [2]

32. a) A choropleth map. [1]

b) i) Area A. [1]

ii) The choropleth map uses categories so we only know that there were 0–20 visitors. [1]

This page has been left blank

Revision Tips

Rethink Revision

Have you ever taken part in a quiz and thought '*I know this*!', but no matter how hard you scrabbled around in your brain you just couldn't come up with the answer?

It's very frustrating when this happens, but in a fun situation it doesn't really matter. However, in tests and assessments, it is essential that you can recall the relevant information when you need to.

Most students think that revision is about making sure you **know** *stuff*, but it is also about being confident that you can **retain** that *stuff* over time and **recall** it when needed.

Revision that Really Works

Experts have found that there are two techniques that help with *all* of these things and consistently produce better results in tests and exams compared to other revision techniques.

Applying these techniques to your KS3 revision will ensure you get better results in tests and assessments and will have all the relevant knowledge at your fingertips when you start studying for your GCSEs.

It really isn't rocket science either – you simply need to:

- **test yourself** on each topic as many times as possible
- **leave a gap** between the test sessions.

It is most effective if you leave a good period of time between the test sessions, e.g. between a week and a month. The idea is that just as you start to forget the information, you force yourself to recall it again, keeping it fresh in your mind.

Three Essential Revision Tips

1 **Use Your Time Wisely**
- Allow yourself plenty of time
- Try to start revising six months before tests and assessments – it's more effective and less stressful
- Your revision time is precious so use it wisely – using the techniques described on this page will ensure you revise effectively and efficiently and get the best results
- Don't waste time re-reading the same information over and over again – it's time-consuming and not effective!

2 **Make a Plan**
- Identify all the topics you need to revise (this Complete Revision & Practice book will help you)
- Plan at least five sessions for each topic
- A one-hour session should be ample to test yourself on the key ideas for a topic
- Spread out the practice sessions for each topic – the optimum time to leave between each session is about one month but, if this isn't possible, just make the gaps as big as realistically possible.

3 **Test Yourself**
- Methods for testing yourself include: quizzes, practice questions, flashcards, past-papers, explaining a topic to someone else, etc.
- This Complete Revision & Practice book gives you seven practice test opportunities per topic
- Don't worry if you get an answer wrong – provided you check what the right answer is, you are more likely to get the same or similar questions right in future!

Visit our website to download your free flashcards, for more information about the benefits of these revision techniques and for further guidance on how to plan ahead and make them work for you.

www.collins.co.uk/collinsks3revision